TAROT

A GUIDED WORKBOOK
TO UNLOCK AND EXPLORE YOUR
MAGICKAL INTUITION

JUDGEMENT

THE SUN.

STRENGTH.

chartwell
books

ᴵᴺTRODUCTION

Tarot cards have been around for centuries in various forms. Over the past six hundred years, people have consulted the cards for religious instruction, spiritual insight, self-knowledge, and divining the future. Think of tarot as a system of archetypes, a picture-book of the human condition, reflecting our states of mind and stages of life.

The basic methodology for tarot is simple. It draws on our innate ability to make connections, recognize ourselves in the stories around us, and reinterpret signs with meaning. The magic in your amazing, imaginative brain can bridge the gap between the archetypes presented on the cards and the events or elements of your own life that your intuition brings to the surface while you work with the cards. Trust that your perceptive powers are revealing the most relevant and important connections through the cards, but pay attention. That doesn't always mean your gut interpretations are right; try to set aside what you *want* to see and then reflect on all sides and potential interpretations.

What matters is that you focus on yourself, the card or cards in front of you, and let the truth flow through you. As long as you are being truthful about what you feel and telling that truth to yourself, then that is what matters.

How to Work with This Book

The pages here offer the basics of what you need to know to read tarot cards for daily affirmation and intuitive or spiritual development. Anyone can learn to work with tarot and can benefit greatly from its insights; all you need is an open mind and a willingness to trust the impressions you sense during a reading. The aim is to help you be creative with tarot, to experiment, and to find ways to read the cards that work for you.

In the first part of this book, you'll learn what the individual cards mean. You may certainly go "in order," but a large part of tarot is relying on your intuition, so flip around and land on a page that feels right to you. Think about the card and follow the prompts to discover more about yourself. You do not need a deck of tarot cards to work in this part of the book.

The second part of the book goes into spreads and readings; for these, you will want to get a deck of your own cards. The number one rule with tarot cards is to treat them respectfully. Don't use them to play games or share them with people who are disrespectful to them. If you take good care of your deck of cards, they can be an easy and accessible tool for tuning in to your intuition whenever you need a little guidance.

Your skills with tarot will grow with a familiarity with both the deck and your relationship to yourself. The answers that a tarot practice bring are highly dependent on your interpretation. A beginner's best approach is to look for guidance through a problem, not specific answers to specific questions. Spend some time focusing on yourself, call your intuition, and connect with the question on your mind.

Quick Reference Guide

0 THE FOOL....................................... beginnings; risks

I THE MAGICIAN.............................. action; ambition; and manifesting

II THE HIGH PRIESTESS .... secrets; intuition; and learning

III THE EMPRESS .... creativity; resources; motherhood

IV THE EMPEROR............................. order; power; and boundaries

V THE HIEROPHANT .... unity; marriage; and education

VI THE LOVERS................................. love; decisions

VII THE CHARIOT............................. progress; determination

VIII STRENGTH .... management; endurance

IX THE HERMIT................................. analysis; solitude

X THE WHEEL OF FORTUNE......... luck; fate

XI JUSTICE. .... decisions; balance; legal affairs

XII THE HANGED MAN.................... waiting; sacrifice

XIII DEATH.. transformation; change; and new beginnings

XIV TEMPERANCE .... negotiation; moderation

XV THE DEVIL................................... restriction; manipulation

XVI THE TOWER............................... breakdown; illumination

XVII THE STAR .... hope;guidance

XVIII THE MOON .... crisis of faith; deep emotions

XIX THE SUN..................................... growth;recovery

XX JUDGEMENT .... the past; second chances

XXI THE WORLD .... success; completion

CUPS

ACE......... love; fertility; beginnings
TWO .... partnerships; relationships
THREE ..... celebration; community
FOUR ...... boredom; stasis
FIVE .... loss; sadness
SIX .... peace; a visitor
SEVEN ..... confusion; possibilities
EIGHT ..... departure; abandonment
NINE .... a wish come true; abundance
TEN......... happiness; family
PAGE....... fun; socializing
KNIGHT... a dreamer; a proposal
QUEEN.... an intuitive woman; sensitivity
KING .... a warmhearted man; support

SWORDS

ACE......... success; clarity
TWO .... stalemate; choice
THREE ..... heartbreak; grief
FOUR ...... rest; recharge
FIVE .... conflict; defeat
SIX .... leaving conflict behind; transition
SEVEN ..... theft; deception
EIGHT ..... restriction; feeling trapped
NINE .... anxiety; fears
TEN......... endings; suffering
PAGE....... gossip; contracts
KNIGHT... battles; an opponent
QUEEN.... an independent woman; knowledge
KING .... a strong-willed man; divorce

PENTACLES

ACE......... money; success; beginnings
TWO .... decisions; balance
THREE ..... showing your talent; collaboration
FOUR ...... stability; money management
FIVE .... financial loss; exclusion
SIX .... generosity; charity
SEVEN ..... potential for success; perserverance
EIGHT ..... money coming; skills
NINE .... material comforts; success
TEN......... inheritance; good business; marriage
PAGE....... an offer; management
KNIGHT... a dependable man; trustworthy
QUEEN.... a generous woman; support
KING .... a prosperous man; security

WANDS

ACE......... news; male fertility; beginnings
TWO .... making plans; on the move
THREE ..... travel; activity
FOUR ...... a holiday; celebration
FIVE .... strong opinions; competition
SIX .... victory; success
SEVEN ..... advocacy; standing strong
EIGHT ..... news; swiftly moving
NINE .... strength; perserverance
TEN......... a burden; feeling overwhelmed
PAGE....... a message; enthusiasm
KNIGHT... speed; an offer
QUEEN.... a creative woman; confidence
KING .... a creative man; motivational

THE CARDS

A standard tarot deck has seventy-eight cards, divided into two groups: twenty-two major arcana cards and fifty-six minor arcana cards. The word *arcana* means secret. The Major Arcana contains all the traditional pictorial cards that are so evocative and commonly associated with tarot: the Fool, Empress, the Lovers, the Devil, plus so many more. The major arcana denote important life events or shifts, while the minor arcana cards reflect day-to-day events and can be seen as more detailed aspects of the major arcana cards. The minor arcana cards are sorted into suites just like a deck of playing cards; the four suites are the wands, pentacles, swords, and cups, each containing an ace, cards two through ten, and "royal" face cards.

Further, every card is like a coin; it has two sides that represent the duality of all our experiences and what we can learn from them. When the card is turned upside down, it is called a reversal. While the meaning is often a more intense interpretation of the upright card, it can sometimes mean the opposite. Each of our lives contain both wonderful and difficult moments, and that's unavoidable. The cards can help us to see and understand the lessons in those experiences and move forward.

THE MAJOR ARCANA

If the tarot were a professional sport, these cards would be the big league. These twenty-two cards represent archetypes drawn from mythology and medieval society.

Given their status, and the fact that they are sometimes referred to as "trump" cards, these cards will more often concern deeper, more life-impacting matters. Although they can be read for their individual meanings, they can also be seen as part of a larger, even mythic journey.

The major arcana cards deal with the major themes of our lives: big choices and decisions, major moments and themes, and examinations that require deep reflections. These powerful images move in a cycle, starting with a new soul at the start of something and ending with the whole world.

Each card is numbered from I to XXI, with The Fool as zero. What follows are some of the most common attributes associated with them and some suggestions for how you can think through their implications. Don't think of these descriptions as definitions or sure things. They are more like jumping-off points, the starting point of a journey into your inner self and your possible futures. This is a journey we all embark on, and each card in the major arcana asks you to reflect on the various celebrations and challenges that each of us face as we move through our lives.

0 THE FOOL

JUMP INTO THE UNKNOWN

Keywords: Beginnings; Risks

The world is full of risk. But wonders, too. As the first card at the beginning of the journey, this is a card of rebirth. The Fool signifies new opportunities. It's never too late to start fresh and follow your heart's desire. It's time for optimism and a fresh perspective. There might be bumps along the way, but take a leap of faith and whatever you start now will go well. Step on out. The world is waiting. But remember! This is a wild card.

What feelings does this card evoke in you? Are you a free spirit? Impulsive?
The life of the party?

_____

_____

_____

_____

How do you feel about risks? Are there times that you feel better about taking them?
Is there something new or risky that lies ahead of you?

_____

_____

_____

_____

Think about a time you took a risk or started something new that worked out. What did
you learn from that experience that you can apply to what lies in front of you?

_____

_____

_____

_____

Reversal: Are you proposing a leap too far? Don't be rash. The reversed Fool leaps
without awareness and so becomes the literal idiot, sabotaging his changes due to
desperation and irrationality.

_____

_____

_____

_____

I THE MAGICIAN

MAKE YOUR OWN MAGIC

Keywords: Action; Ambition; Manifesting

With all the tools you need at your disposal, the Magician represents creation, potential, and manifestation. This is the card of the inventor, the self-employed, the entrepreneur, the side-hustler. You will have the drive to spur your plans forward and take new, creative approaches: to think laterally, ask questions, trust your internal guidance, and let go of procrastination. Ground yourself but keep an eye on what is coming, as something previously hidden could be coming to light. Make the most of your skills and talents and step into your power; focus on your projects and capitalize on your personal strengths.

What feelings does this card evoke in you? Are you confident? In control?

_____

_____

_____

What are your greatest skills or assets? How can you use them to achieve your current goal?

_____

_____

_____

If you don't feel powerful, successful, or confident at this time, think about someone you know who generally is and how they achieve their goals. How can you emulate them?

_____

_____

_____

Is it time to open yourself to possibilities? Do you have untapped potential?

_____

_____

_____

Reversal: The reversed Magician turns trickster, so this card can show you being misled by a charming manipulator. What you see is not what you get, and it's all show, not truth. It can also reveal a creative block, delays, and miscommunication in general. Are you feeling blocked or misunderstood?

_____

_____

_____

II THE HIGH PRIESTESS

EXPLORE YOUR SPIRITUAL SIDE

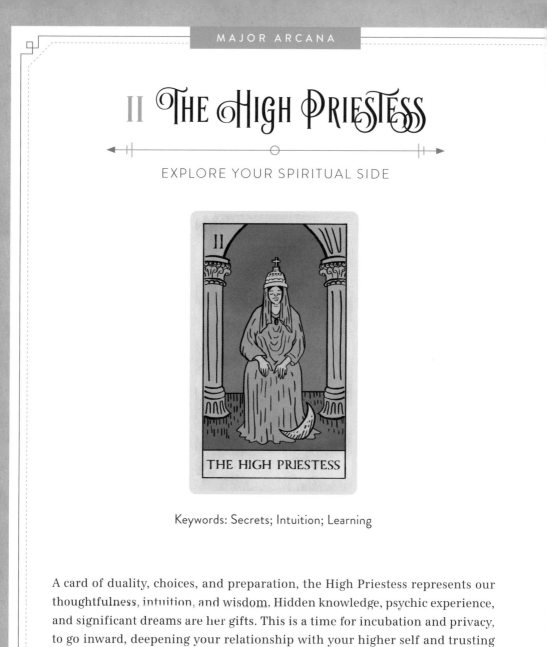

THE HIGH PRIESTESS

Keywords: Secrets; Intuition; Learning

A card of duality, choices, and preparation, the High Priestess represents our thoughtfulness, intuition, and wisdom. Hidden knowledge, psychic experience, and significant dreams are her gifts. This is a time for incubation and privacy, to go inward, deepening your relationship with your higher self and trusting your internal voice—but you may not listen to it as much as you should. In your everyday life, confidentiality is key. If you have a secret, or a project you are nurturing, it is better to keep your own counsel.

What feelings does this card evoke in you? Do seem to always know when someone needs you? Do you tend to follow your "gut"? Do others look to you as a confidant?

_____

_____

_____

_____

Think about a time when you trusted your gut rather than listening to the advice of others. Are you facing something now where paying attention to your intuition might be an advantage?

_____

_____

_____

Have you met someone recently who gave you strong feelings, either positive or negative? Did you acknowledge those feelings? If some time has passed, have you assessed whether your feelings panned out?

_____

_____

_____

Reversal: The reversed High Priestess can show an inappropriate mentor or someone trying to persuade you to go against your intuition. Have you recently followed bad advice, or do you think you might be choosing a wrong path? It can also indicate secrets that need to be out in the open. Is there anything you might be holding on to that may be potentially harmful?

_____

_____

_____

_____

III THE EMPRESS

BE YOUR OWN FAIRY GODMOTHER

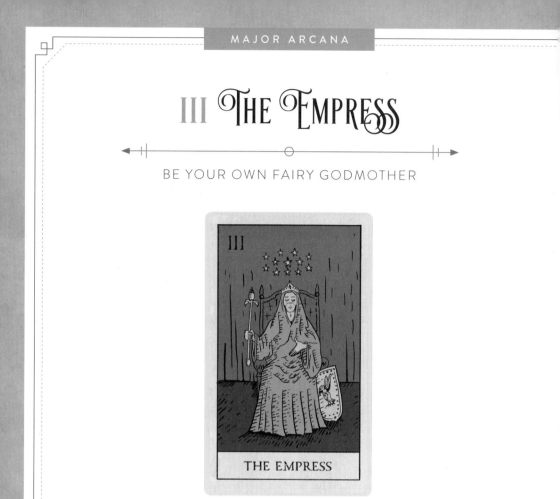

THE EMPRESS

Keywords: Creativity; Resources; Motherhood

Abundant and collaborative, this card embodies growth, divinity, celebration, and evolution. The gifts of the Empress are abundance and material comfort, sensuality and security, and emotional support. The Empress symbolizes fertility and femininity. Your creative projects thrive and you prosper financially. The Empress is resourceful, so you can feel assured that your needs will be met. This card, therefore, shows the influence of a nurturing mother figure who supports you.

What feelings does this card evoke in you? Do you feel as if you've being rewarded for your efforts? Why or why not?

_____

_____

_____

_____

How do you use your many gifts? What have you given to others? What have they given to you?

_____

_____

_____

Is there a project or situation in your future—or even a current relationship—that requires your attention, creativity, and nurturing to thrive? What are some things you can do to bring about the best outcome?

_____

_____

_____

Reversal: The reversed Empress shows money troubles and relationship and domestic issues. She can also show someone who is needy and takes too much from you. The result of these challenges and demands is stressful, which may impact your creativity and productivity. Are there current challenges that are getting in the way of your productivity?

_____

_____

_____

_____

IV THE EMPEROR

DON'T APOLOGIZE FOR WHO YOU ARE

Keywords: Order; Power; Boundaries

This card represents stability, structure, and responsibility. The Emperor can denote a powerful man (and the traditionally male aspects of power, authority, and ambition). He signifies an intimate partner who is constant and trustworthy, in control of his emotions, and comfortable with who he is. He brings balance, security, and conventional values. He shows a return to order (or a sign of improvement in your circumstances). Use your wisdom, determination, and skills to bring order to chaos; trust yourself to make the right decisions. But remember: even though a ruler has a throne, a ruler still serves.

What feelings does this card evoke in you? Do you feel as if you are generally in control of your emotions?

_____

_____

_____

_____

Consider the words stability, power, and authority and whether they apply to you. Do they have good or bad connotations?

_____

_____

_____

_____

Is there a certain type of person or situation where you might try to force your will or take control?

_____

_____

_____

Reversal: The reversed Emperor is power-hungry, demanding, greedy, and ego driven. Talk about toxic masculinity! He does not know where to draw the line and may use excessive force or persuasion to get what he wants. Are you experiencing issues with authority figures and other potentially domineering individuals?

_____

_____

_____

_____

V THE HIEROPHANT

DEVELOP YOURSELF EMOTIONALLY AND SPIRITUALLY

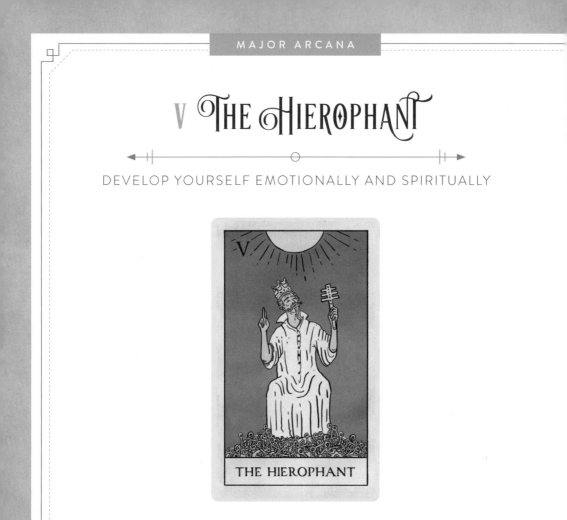

Keywords: Unity; Marriage; Education

An authority figure and intermediary between the material and spirit, the Hierophant embodies guidance, teaching, and intention. This card shows support, self-realization, and expansion. This is a time to commit to relationships; think and philosophize; take a class, join a study group, or become more spiritually aware. Nurture your talents through learning and heeding good advice. Additionally, the Hierophant represents institutions and traditional values—which may be a comfort to you or a test of how much you are willing to conform. You could be on the verge of attaining knowledge, wisdom, and blessing.

What feelings does this card evoke in you? Is there something new you've been wanting to try or study? What's been holding you back?

_____

_____

_____

_____

The Hierophant offers an opportunity to question and define your values. Have you noticed a shift in something you always valued? What might have changed?

_____

_____

_____

_____

Think of a teacher or leader you've had. What about them inspired you? Do you use those same qualities when you're interacting with others?

_____

_____

_____

_____

Reversal: The reversed Hierophant shows poor leadership, the judgmental teacher who is more interested in furthering his ambitions than supporting you. In work, it can show institutions that need restructuring. It is better to seek your own path than to stay with a mentor or plan that doesn't suit your needs. Is there someone or something that may be standing in your way?

_____

_____

_____

VI THE LOVERS

FOLLOW YOUR HEART

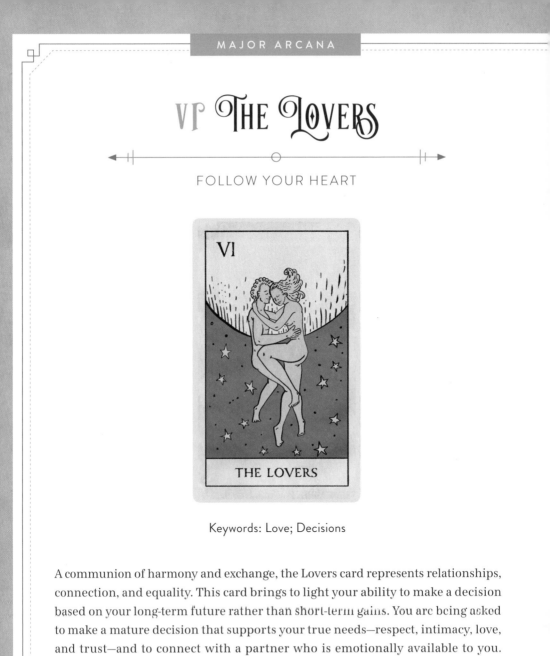

Keywords: Love; Decisions

A communion of harmony and exchange, the Lovers card represents relationships, connection, and equality. This card brings to light your ability to make a decision based on your long-term future rather than short-term gains. You are being asked to make a mature decision that supports your true needs—respect, intimacy, love, and trust—and to connect with a partner who is emotionally available to you. The card can predict meeting a new partner or a career opportunity, and your choice will have a significant effect on your future. There is reason for optimism and the potential for harmony.

What feelings does this card evoke in you? Do you feel that you're more of an idealist when it comes to relationships, or are you more grounded?

_____

_____

_____

_____

If you are in a relationship, you might need to decide whether to take your partnership to a deeper level. What might that deeper level look like?

_____

_____

_____

_____

You could be on the verge of overcoming an obstacle. What do you think it is, and what will you have to do?

_____

_____

_____

Reversal: The reversed Lovers suggests a relationship in crisis. The shadow side of your personalities enters the equation, and you may question your initial attraction. There may be inequality, betrayal, and dishonesty or lust, materialism, and addiction to negative patterns. Have you been feeling out of balance with your partner? What's shifted in your relationship?

_____

_____

_____

_____

VII THE CHARIOT

PERSEVERE AGAINST ALL ODDS

Keywords: Progress; Determination

The Chariot is a celebration of individuality, victory, transition, and overcoming obstacles. It signifies success and a major departure. This is a time for determination and focus as you travel in a new direction. A decision is made, and now you can begin to experience real progress! You are ready to take control and learn as your horizons rapidly expand. The Chariot can indicate a move or an important journey, and, on a mundane level, it represents a road trip or perhaps getting a new vehicle. Keep in mind that the journey can be just as important as the destination.

What feelings does this card evoke in you? Do you consider yourself determined, or do you easily give up—or is there a place and a time for each?

_____

_____

_____

_____

Is there a journey or move ahead of you? What are some potential pitfalls, and what are some things you can do to gain courage and confidence?

_____

_____

_____

_____

A significant detour may be coming. Are you going to fight your way through or go around? Do you know what your ultimate goal is? How are you going to get there?

_____

_____

_____

_____

Reversal: The reversed Chariot signals arrogance and self-indulgence. This can show a person or event spiraling out of control. Ego is at work, and selfish needs come before the greater good. It can also cancel or delay travel plans and house moves. Have you stood in your own way recently? Explore why that was.

_____

_____

_____

VIII STRENGTH

YOU ARE CAPABLE

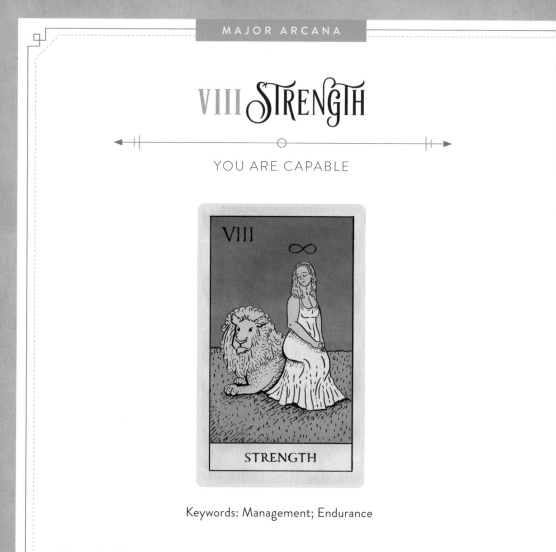

Keywords: Management; Endurance

The embodiment of Strength is patience, working with limitation, and striving toward perfection. The Strength card represents self-guidance and self-confidence. It's time to summon your courage and determination to get the situation under control. Remember to act with grace and sensitivity rather than using brute force. This is a good card for leadership, as it signifies you are ready to take on a challenge and stand firm. See this as victory or triumph, but it is also potentially a place of thoughtfulness and compassion for others. There is confidence in strength, a feeling of permanence and solidity.

What feelings does this card evoke in you? What does strength mean for you?

_____

_____

_____

_____

In creative projects, Strength shows you taking a raw idea and developing it without sacrificing its spirit. Think about raw idea or concept you may have and how it could take physical form as a piece of artwork, writing, or prototype.

_____

_____

_____

In terms of health, Strength shows resilience and vitality, recovery from illness, and the willpower to break bad habits. Are there any bad habits you've been wanting to break, and what are some things you can do to make that happen?

_____

_____

_____

Reversal: When reversed, the Strength card represents weakness of will and avoidance of risk, conflicts, and decision-making. This can refer to you ignoring your instincts altogether or allowing fear of conflict to stop you from taking action. What are some ways you can step up to the plate and take action?

_____

_____

_____

_____

IX THE HERMIT

TAKE SOME "ME TIME"

Keywords: Analysis; Solitude

Often associated with isolation, the Hermit celebrates forging your own path and the pursuit of truth and knowledge. This card most commonly represents a state of mind in which you wisely withdraw and keep your own counsel, enjoying solitude, as you need space to process your thoughts and feelings. It can show breaking with tradition and finding a unique approach to a challenge. Rely on yourself, as you have the answers you need. If you are under pressure to make a decision, the Hermit shows you need more time.

What feelings does this card evoke in you? Do you enjoy a bit of solitude, or do you dread it?

_____

_____

_____

_____

Do you feel the need to fill silences with idle chatter or electronics or some other mental stimulation? Why do you think that is?

_____

_____

_____

_____

There's a difference between choosing solitude and being lonely, not by choice. Can you think of someone in your life who may need a friend or connection right now?

_____

_____

_____

_____

Reversal: The reversed Hermit may indicate you're feeling alone and unsupported; this is more an attitude than reality, so ask yourself if you're avoiding help. Alternatively, the card can show a time when you're cut off from your usual support systems or have been ghosted by those you trusted. Think of a time you've felt excluded and write about those emotions.

_____

_____

_____

_____

X THE WHEEL OF FORTUNE

SPIN THAT WHEEL LIKE YOU MEAN IT

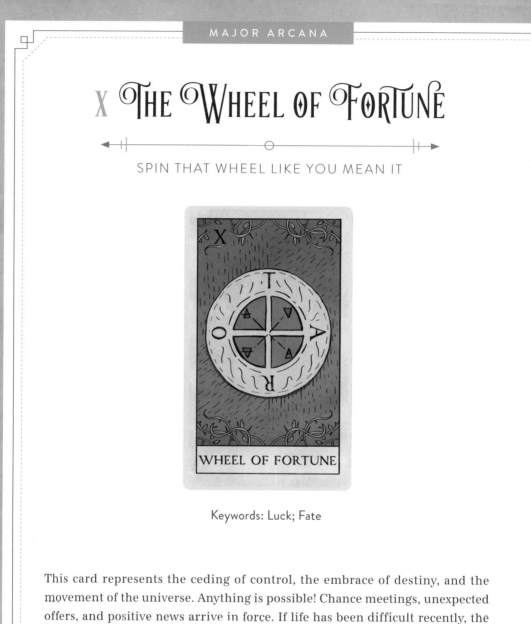

Keywords: Luck; Fate

This card represents the ceding of control, the embrace of destiny, and the movement of the universe. Anything is possible! Chance meetings, unexpected offers, and positive news arrive in force. If life has been difficult recently, the Wheel shows a turn for the better. Additionally, it reveals psychic ability, so use it wisely to listen to your intuition and manifest your wishes. While you cannot control the forces of the universe, you can certainly come to a better understanding of your role within it.

What feelings does this card evoke in you? Do you think of yourself as lucky, always in the right place at the right time?

_____

_____

_____

_____

Think of a time when you seemed on a streak of bad luck. How did you cope with that, and what did you learn from the experience?

_____

_____

_____

_____

Would people describe you as moody or temperamental, up one day and down the next? Are these mood fluctuations reactions to what's going on around you?

_____

_____

_____

Reversal: When the Wheel is reversed, you may suffer some bad luck, but thankfully this marks the end of a run of challenges. In this way, the reversed Wheel represents closure. Vow to adapt, begin again, and keep on working toward your goal. What is your goal?

_____

_____

_____

_____

XI JUSTICE

YOU CAN'T RUN FROM KARMA

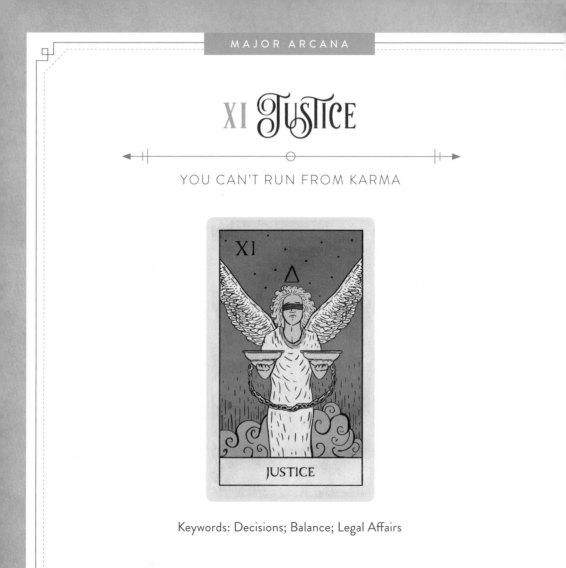

Keywords: Decisions; Balance; Legal Affairs

A card concerned with consequences, Justice represents the balance of relationships, the ebb and flow of power. This is a time when past errors or imbalances can be redressed. Or you may be your own judge, using your perspective and integrity to make good decisions that will safeguard your future. You may take a moral stand on an issue. In legal matters, a decision is made in your favor. Justice shows a logical, considered influence—a welcome arrival if life has felt chaotic. It is a card of empowerment, advising you to take a left-brain approach to take control.

What feelings does this card evoke in you? Do you consider yourself to be fair and unbiased? Is it only in certain situations?

_____

_____

_____

On a spiritual level, Justice shows the working out of karma, or actions and consequences. Is there a time when you did something bad, only to have something bad happen to you? How about something good?

_____

_____

_____

Now is a time for your projects to get support. Listen to advice from people around you whom you respect. What are some ideas you have, and have you sought advice? Do you think your hard work will be rewarded?

_____

_____

_____

Reversal: With reversed Justice, life goes out of balance. Work, relationships, and money issues spiral out of control. You are treated unfairly, which is compounded by bad advice from a trusted individual. You are not able to speak your truth and feel overruled by those who don't understand your predicament. Find your voice and stay strong to your values. Write them down here.

_____

_____

_____

_____

XII THE HANGED MAN

CHANGE YOUR PERSPECTIVE

Keywords: Waiting; Sacrifice

The Hanged Man is a pause, inner reflection, and patience. The obvious meaning of the card is hanging around: Events are not moving with speed, but all you can do is wait, knowing the universe has a plan. The card can also indicate that you've made sacrifices and are eager to see rewards. There are a lot of factors that are beyond your control, so sit back and relax as you can expect delays. Creatively, this card can appear when you're feeling frustrated with your progress. However, the Hanged Man's message is incubation—your project needs time to evolve.

What feelings does this card evoke in you? In what ways do you display patience?

_____

_____

_____

_____

Sometimes things look worse than they are. Try to look at a current challenge from a newer, fresher angle. What do you see?

_____

_____

_____

_____

Is there someone in your life who makes no sacrifices or concessions? Is it you sometimes? Is it possible others could benefit from even a small sacrifice, selflessly made?

_____

_____

_____

_____

Reversal: The reversed Hanged Man can be a sign of rigid thinking and martyrdom. You may need to revise your expectations. Are you hanging on to a fantasy that may make you a victim rather than a victor? Take another view and liberate yourself from an obligation that cannot offer you what you want.

_____

_____

_____

_____

XIII ⅅEATH

DON'T FEAR THE REAPER

Keywords: Transformation; Change; New Beginnings

This card represents the natural cycles of life, both fertility and fallowness, and rebirth. Death brings endings and beginnings sometimes all at once. This a time of fast and deep transformation and an opportunity to let go of whatever you no longer need. The changes indicated by the Death card can be sudden and shocking. A break with the past—from relationships, friendships, jobs that are no longer satisfying—is the only way forward. In this sense, Death can be a release and a relief, leaving you with the bare bones, the truth.

What feelings does this card evoke in you? Does this card frighten you, or are you excited by the possibilities?

_____

_____

_____

_____

If something is coming to an end in your life, it might be a significant change but it also might not be anything to be afraid of. Are you ready for a new chapter? Even if the answer is no, how can you prepare for it?

_____

_____

_____

You have little control over events when Death looms, but in time you'll see this change in circumstances as a blessing. In what ways do you fight or postpone change? Would accepting it feel more liberating?

_____

_____

_____

Reversal: Death reversed has virtually the same meaning as the card in the upright position. You may feel anxious and stressed, unable to comprehend what is happening. The universe is telling you that there is no way back—a relationship cannot be mended, an employer won't change their mind. Is there something in your life that you know has come to a close but you can't let it go?

_____

_____

XIV° TEMPERANCE

FIND BALANCE

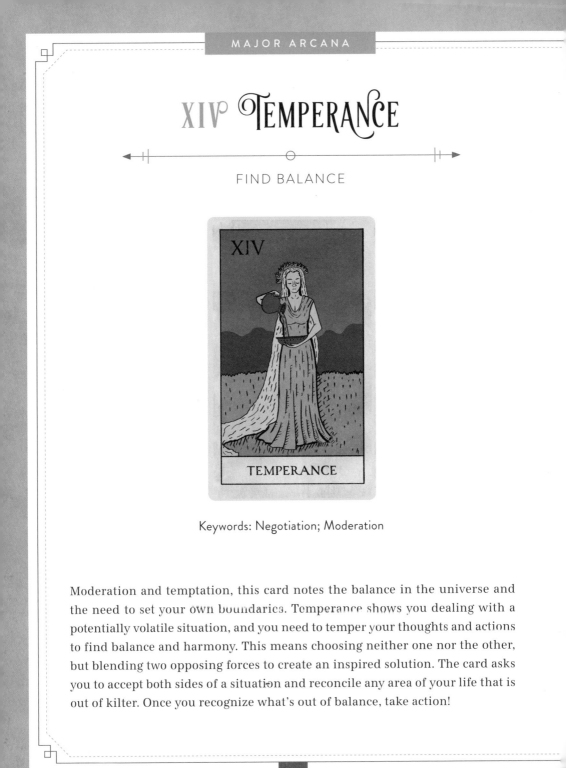

Keywords: Negotiation; Moderation

Moderation and temptation, this card notes the balance in the universe and the need to set your own boundaries. Temperance shows you dealing with a potentially volatile situation, and you need to temper your thoughts and actions to find balance and harmony. This means choosing neither one nor the other, but blending two opposing forces to create an inspired solution. The card asks you to accept both sides of a situation and reconcile any area of your life that is out of kilter. Once you recognize what's out of balance, take action!

What feelings does this card evoke in you? Do you practice moderation or otherwise try to find common ground?

_____

_____

_____

Do you know someone who seems to have a good work-life balance? How do you think they do it? What could you try?

_____

_____

_____

There is a time to commit yourself fully and a time to hang back. Where have you been putting your time and energy lately?

_____

_____

_____

What have you been ignoring or not attending to?

_____

_____

_____

Reversal: Temperance reversed shows imbalance and unfairness in relationships and problems with money. This card can also show you struggling with change, and the past dominating your present and future. In this position, difficult old memories can resurface and you feel held back. What do you need now, in the present?

_____

_____

_____

XV THE DEVIL

KICK NEGATIVITY TO THE CURB

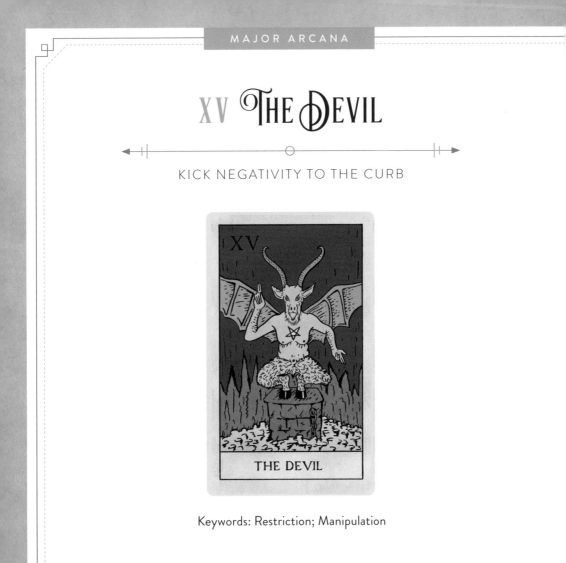

Keywords: Restriction; Manipulation

Instability and power inform the meaning of the Devil, exposing relationships to authority and loss. You may be enslaved to a situation or relationship that demands too much, or you may be feeling controlled and under a bad influence. What started positively has reversed, and now you see it for what it is. This card often describes situations that aren't worth trying to fix; it's a card of greed, temptation, and materialism. The message is to simply walk away, regardless of the temptation to stay. Yet to change the situation, you will need to use a little devilish cunning.

If you're in a toxic relationship or situation, what's stopping you from walking away?

_____

_____

_____

_____

Is there someone in your life who has negative influence over you? Do you feel manipulated, or charmed?

_____

_____

_____

_____

The Devil can show lust and negative ways of relating, in that one partner is gaining much more that the other. Additional meanings include issues with sex, food, or substance abuse. Is there an unbalanced desire in your life right now?

_____

_____

_____

Reversal: The reversed Devil is one of the few cards whose meaning becomes more hopeful. It suggests the decision you need to make will be easier than you think. Now is the time to make your move and banish those toxic situations. Is there something you've been contemplating, and does the decision seem clearer now?

_____

_____

_____

_____

XVI THE TOWER

EMBRACE THE CHAOS

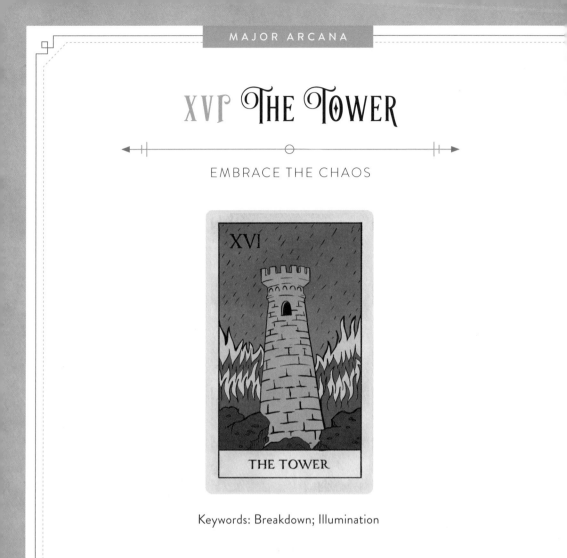

Keywords: Breakdown; Illumination

This card is the manifestation of imbalance and surprise disruption, leading the way into new paths. The Tower hits us with sudden change—the collapse of an ideal, a dream, an organization, or a relationship—that's inevitable and due to forces beyond our control. The Tower can represent shattered ego, so you may feel vulnerable and confused. Surrender to its power and accept the huge shift in awareness it offers, even if the benefits aren't obvious yet. The upside is its message of release. The walls come tumbling down, and what you build next can have more foundation.

What feelings does this card evoke in you? Do you feel protective of things and fear change?

_____

_____

_____

_____

Think of the story of the Three Little Pigs. Is there a relationship in your life that feels unstable, like the house made of straw or sticks, where just a little puff might knock it down?

_____

_____

_____

_____

Are you sometimes like the Tower—unpredictable, liable to fall apart or blow up when pushed too far? What situations cause that reaction?

_____

_____

_____

_____

Reversal: When the Tower is reversed, you may find yourself taking responsibility even when you are blameless. It can also show you have held on to a career, project, or relationship that isn't strong enough to stand the test of time. Have you taken blame for something, or are you holding on to something you should let go?

_____

_____

_____

_____

XVII THE STAR

GO AHEAD AND WISH UPON A STAR

Keywords: Hope; Guidance

Individuality and confidence fuel expression and creativity, allowing you to flourish. The Star offers hope and guidance, so if things have felt difficult recently, have faith that your luck is about to change for the better. The Star is a powerful symbol of hope, and you can begin to appreciate everything life has to offer. The Star supports beauty, creativity, and sharing your love, gifts, and talents. It allows you to shine. The Star also shows good health. It is the card of the healer.

What feelings does this card evoke in you? Do you feel you're a hopeful person? What beliefs keep you going?

_____

_____

_____

_____

There's a saying that to plant a garden is to believe in tomorrow. Is there a project you've been wanting to start, that you can do today?

_____

_____

_____

_____

Think of someone you know who always seems full of hope. How do you think they're able to look past difficulties and still have a positive outlook?

_____

_____

_____

_____

Reversal: The reversed Star can suggest you're giving up too easily in your projects and experiencing a creative block. An additional meaning is feeling alone, without the support you need. Is there something you've set aside, unable to finish?

_____

_____

_____

_____

XVIII THE MOON

DIG DEEPER

Keywords: Crisis of Faith; Deep Emotions

This card represents instinct and intuition, the power of dreams, and the potential pitfalls of illusions. The Moon's traditional meaning is a period of emotional vulnerability. It reveals misgivings about a situation, as you cannot be sure if what you're seeing is the truth. This may be a time of deep emotional conflict, and the struggle is private rather than shared. You have a decision to make, and to choose wisely, take note of your intuitive messages and dreams. The prospect may make you uncomfortable, but the Moon asks you to dive deep and examine the real cause of conflict.

What feelings does this card evoke in you? Do you feel vulnerable or have misgivings about something?

_____

_____

_____

_____

Under the light of the Moon, is what you are seeing an illusion? Or does the Moon bring to light the essence of a problem that needs attention?

_____

_____

_____

_____

Do you sometimes wear masks to cover your emotions? With certain people? All the time?

_____

_____

_____

_____

Reversal: The reversed Moon may show you avoiding difficult emotions and confrontations because your needs are not expressed or recognized. A trauma is ignored rather than explored, so the Moon reversed can show you going back to old habits of coping with the past. Is there something you've been ignoring, and what are some new ways you can cope with it?

_____

_____

_____

_____

XIX THE SUN

SHINE ON!

THE SUN

Keywords: Growth; Recovery

The embodiment of illumination and openness, this card reveals the stark reality of your path. The Sun brings success and achievement and is one of the most positive cards. If you've had a challenging time, it shows that every aspect of your life will improve. You'll also enjoy more energy, and if you or someone close has suffered from health problems, the card predicts recovery. As a card of energy and growth, all your projects benefit now, so the Sun heralds a good time to nurture your creative endeavors, your business, and the relationships you value.

What feelings does this card evoke in you? Does it inspire happiness?

_____

_____

_____

_____

Is there something in your life that you've been hoping will improve? How optimistic are you that it will?

_____

_____

_____

_____

Do you feel strong and healthy? If not, what are some things you can do to turn that around?

_____

_____

_____

_____

Reversal: It's virtually impossible to see any negative side to the sun, even when reversed. The only glitch could be a delay to travel plans, but you will enjoy a happy and content period regardless. Write about a happy period in your life, either in the past or still to come.

_____

_____

_____

_____

_____

XX JUDGMENT

BE SELF-AWARE RATHER THAN SELF-CRITICAL

Keywords: The Past; Second Chances

Both an end and a beginning, Judgment requests that you consider your choices and their consequences. Great changes and opportunities are on the horizon, but before you can decide on your direction, certain past issues need to be addressed. This process is all about how you judge yourself on your past actions and attitudes. Judgment shows you will feel you did the best you could. As you accept yourself fully, you can blow your own horn for your achievements. An additional meaning is being in the public eye. You've put yourself out there and opened yourself to others' judgment.

What feelings does this card evoke in you? Do you judge yourself today for your past, or do you remember things more fondly?

_____

_____

_____

_____

Are you critical or judgmental of others? Do those feelings change when more information about their situation comes to light? Should that matter?

_____

_____

_____

_____

What are some ways you can deal with the judgment of others? Does it matter what people think?

_____

_____

_____

_____

Reversal: When Judgment is reversed, you may be stuck in the past or refuse to learn its lessons. Remember: the past cannot be changed, only accepted. Have compassion for the person you were then and for the decisions you made. You don't have to live with the results of these choices in the future. Write about how you can decide to be free.

_____

_____

_____

_____

XXI THE WORLD

FEEL YOUR DESERVED SUCCESS

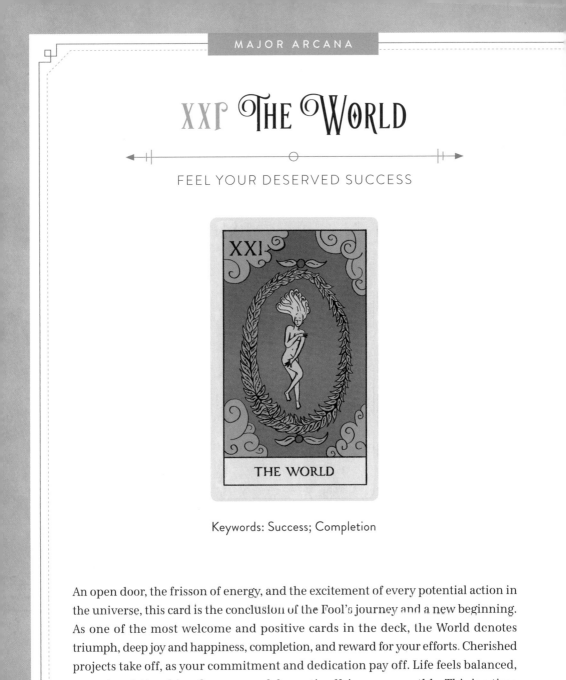

Keywords: Success; Completion

An open door, the frisson of energy, and the excitement of every potential action in the universe, this card is the conclusion of the Fool's journey and a new beginning. As one of the most welcome and positive cards in the deck, the World denotes triumph, deep joy and happiness, completion, and reward for your efforts. Cherished projects take off, as your commitment and dedication pay off. Life feels balanced, as work, relationships, finances, and domestic affairs run smoothly. This is a time for celebration, so it is a great card for groups and positive group consciousness.

What feelings does this card evoke in you? Do things seem to be going your way?

_____

_____

_____

_____

How do you view the completion of a big task? Do you celebrate and look forward to the next thing, or are you mournful?

_____

_____

_____

_____

If you've worked hard to achieve something, are you comfortable basking in that success? Why or why not?

_____

_____

_____

Reversal: The reversed World shows roads blocked, or you don't feel you are deserving of success. It can also show hanging on to one ambition that eludes you—and if so, it's time to redefine what you want and adjust your expectations. Alternatively, you may feel eclipsed by another's shining light. Write about how you can keep the faith until you can get what you deserve.

_____

_____

_____

The Minor Arcana

The minor arcana cards are more numerous, forming the larger portion of the tarot deck. These cards are ordered into four suites, each with their own characteristics dictated by the elements that rule them. Within each suite there is an ace, cards two through ten, and four face cards. Each of these numbered or face cards have their own meanings, following a cycle similar to the Fool's journey, but on a smaller scale. The combined meaning of the number and the suite come together to represent a unique concept for each card. The minor arcana deal in the matters of our lives, the routines, the heartbreaks, the job changes, and ambitions. These moments feel weighty and important, but the contrast between the Majors and Minors is one of lifelong concerns, unfolding over weeks or months, rather than cycles of many years.

What the Suits Mean

CUPS
Ruled by water, the flowing font of emotion and feeling. They also embody intuition, spirituality, as well as relationships and connection. It's a suite that also rules love, beauty, and romance.

PENTACLES
Ruled by earthand concern all material matters. This means the cards will embody money, structure, home, and responsibility. It's a suite concerned with the body, health, and taking care of home and career.

SWORDS
Ruled by air, which embraces the intellect, words, and the whirl of thoughts. They are also associated with conflict, force, and intensity. This suite also concerns anxiety, your ego, and your logic; ask for mental clarity and the need for resolution and decisions.

WANDS
Ruled by fire and are consequently associated with enthusiasm, passion, and creativity. Embody action and energy, the process of learning, talking and creating, and the pursuit of ambition and adventure.

What the Numbers Mean

In numerology, the ancient art of mystical number interpretation, numbers have the following meanings:

ONES (ACES):
Beginnings and new energy; a new cycle of creation, inspiration, and potential

TWOS:
Partnerships, balance, and division; unity and duality, choices, and opposition

THREES:
Acknowledgment; abundant growth, collaboration, and accumulation

FOURS:
Stability and boundaries; structure and stability, building foundations, responsibility

FIVES:
Instability and challenges; progress and transformation, change, and loss

SIXES:
Harmony and improvement; solution and exchange, giving and receiving

SEVENS:
Potential and ambitions; challenges, choices, transitions, and individuality

EIGHTS:
Rewards and progress; pursuit of perfection, strength, limitation, and transcendence

NINES:
Intensity; completion and ripeness, achievement and challenges, a journey's conclusion

TENS:
Culmination, completion, endings, and also beginnings.

And though they're not numbered, here are additional meanings to the face cards:

PAGES:
Receiving of new messages and information, learning and education, apprenticeship, and effort

KNIGHTS:
Action and movement, new ideas and motivation, decisions, consequences, and ego

QUEENS:
Nurturing and fertility, abundance and creativity, growth, care, intuition, flexibility, and fluidity

KINGS:
Leadership and structure, stubbornness and rigidity, willpower, passion, and ambition

Ace of Cups

BREW SOMETHING NEW

Keywords: Love; Fertility; Beginnings

The Ace of Cups brings the gift of love and key emotional events like pregnancy, birth, and motherhood. When not predicting a pregnancy, it can reveal that being a parent and/or partner takes priority over work, finances, and projects. In relationships, the card denotes falling in love, passion, and a significant new partnership. In existing relationships, it signifies loves and support. Positive emotions flow. If you are nurturing a new project, this Ace heralds creativity and growth, so make time for activities you enjoy, and you will see them flourish.

What feelings does this card evoke in you?

_____

_____

_____

_____

Are you open to a new relationship right now, either platonic or romantic?

_____

_____

_____

_____

What are some ways you express your emotions?

_____

_____

_____

_____

Reversal: The reversed Ace suggests fertility issues and creative block. There may be lack of space or time to nurture your relationships and projects, or you may be feeling exhausted due to others' emotional demands. The reversed One can indicate disappointment and confusion in relationships. Are you feeling neglected in a relationship or exhausted by a new project?

_____

_____

_____

_____

_____

TWO OF CUPS

HAVE A HEARTFELT CONNECTIONS

Keywords: Partnerships; Relationships

The Two of Cups represents harmony, peace, partnership, and love. It signifies a deeper commitment in an existing relationship and it also predicts new romance and strong passions, which may be all-consuming just now. Inspiring partnerships are favored too, so this is an auspicious card for getting together with a study partner or anyone with whom you share similar creative interests; the relationship will be mutually supportive and understanding. Nurture all your relationships and enjoy the love and pleasure they bring. As a prediction card, this Two shows deeper love is coming—and you deserve all that is on offer.

What feelings does this card evoke in you?

_____

_____

_____

_____

_____

Is there a friendship that has waned over time? What can you do to rekindle it?

_____

_____

_____

_____

Are you in a situation where you can form a new partnership? What do you bring to the party?

_____

_____

_____

_____

Reversal: The reversed Two reveals relationship stress. The card asks you to rely on your intuition. Though everything may appear to be ticking along, pay attention to your instincts; there's a reason for doubt, and it's time to communicate openly about any fears rather than ignore them. Is there a stressful relationship in your life?

_____

_____

_____

_____

_____

THREE OF CUPS

GET YOUR PARTY ON

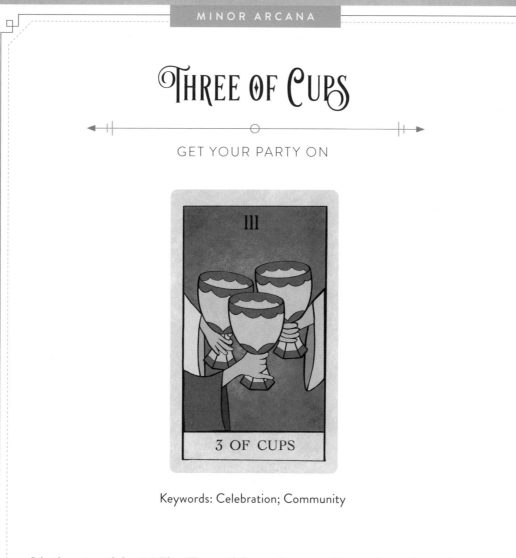

Keywords: Celebration; Community

It's time to celebrate! The Three of Cups shows parties and reunions—from anniversaries, christenings, weddings, and birthdays to a great night out or weekend away with friends and family. This is a time for indulgence and reward, to enjoy others' company, be carefree, and have simple fun. Whatever your pleasure, this Three ultimately reveals emotional and/or physical healing. Spending time with people who make you feel good raises your vibration and energy levels. It's time to let your talent shine.

What feelings does this card evoke in you?

_____

_____

_____

_____

_____

What are some social groups you belong to? Do they serve different needs?

_____

_____

_____

_____

Think of something going on in your life that's worth celebrating.

_____

_____

_____

_____

Reversal: The reversed Three can indicate a flirtation or indulgence gone too far. In established relationships, there may be distance and a lack of cohesion and understanding. Creativity takes a nosedive, too, as creative blocks abound. This card can also show irritating or recurrent health problems. Does any of this ring true right now?

_____

_____

_____

_____

_____

Four of Cups

KICK BOREDOM TO THE CURB

Keywords: Boredom; Stasis

If you're looking for a relationship, the Four of Cups shows disillusion. It often comes up if you've been hurt in the past and protect yourself by rejecting those who don't live up to your standards. It's time to risk opening up emotionally, but there may be some past issues still to heal. This Four shows a tinge of boredom or a static situation, whether in an established relationship or in your work life. Even a small change to your environment will go a long way to making you feel you're going forward, so look around for some much-needed inspiration.

What feelings does this card evoke in you?

_____

_____

_____

_____

Are you feeling bored, stagnant, or apathetic about a situation or person right now?

_____

_____

_____

_____

Does your boredom cause you to get out there and change things, or are you missing opportunities?

_____

_____

_____

_____

Reversal: The reversed Four generally means the same as the upright card, but with a higher degree of dissatisfaction—you may be yearning for change but don't yet know what you want. If so, it's important to try new tactics and address what needs to change in your relationship or work environment. What could those be?

_____

_____

_____

_____

Five of Cups

PICK UP THE PIECES

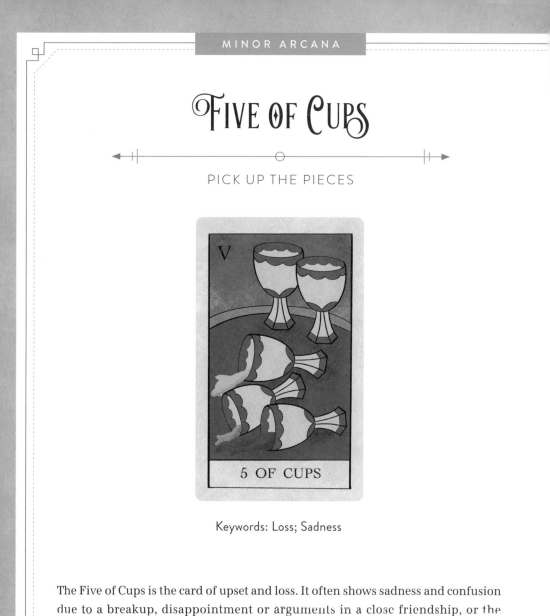

Keywords: Loss; Sadness

The Five of Cups is the card of upset and loss. It often shows sadness and confusion due to a breakup, disappointment or arguments in a close friendship, or the need to temporarily move away from someone who has caused hurt. The card can also apply to leaving a job or home before you're ready, or to a loss of status or money. But all is not lost: you will be able to move onward and upward. This Five also indicates that you're revisiting the past, trying to assimilate old stress and sorrow in order to make a fresh start.

What feelings does this card evoke in you?

_____

_____

_____

_____

Write about your loss or sadness, even if it's just keywords or emotions.

_____

_____

_____

_____

Write a list of some things you have to look forward to.

_____

_____

_____

_____

Reversal: The reversed Five reveals you have already experienced the lowest point in a downward cycle and, as a result, are close to recovery. Ready to pick up the pieces, you will be stronger than you were before, able to face reality and move forward. An additional meaning of the card is meeting up with old friends. Are there painful past memories you're ready to let go of?

_____

_____

_____

_____

Six of Cups

WATCH THE SEEDS OF THE PAST BLOSSOM IN THE PRESENT

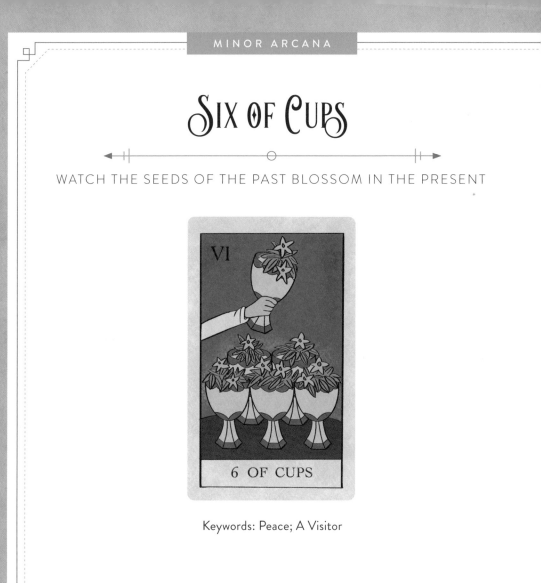

Keywords: Peace; A Visitor

The Six of Cups reveals happy memories, a time to recall childhood with fondness. In some way, the past returns to help you in the present, too, as conversations and reminiscing with old friends may seed a new idea. Overall, you'll find the right balance in relationships and enjoy a period of peace and harmony. This Six also shows compassion and kindness, so sweet, happy times are ahead, and any disruptions or upsets will be soothed and remedied. In love, an old flame comes back, and you may need to weigh whether it's worth going back.

What feelings does this card evoke in you?

_____

_____

_____

_____

Is there a person from your past you've been meaning to reconnect with? Why, and what's been stopping you?

_____

_____

_____

_____

Are there times when you could be more playful, instead of serious?

_____

_____

_____

_____

Reversal: When the Six is reversed, nostalgia rules, and you may recall past events with more positivity than they deserve. The card can show you feeling locked in the past as a way to avoid moving on. Unexpected visitors or communications may stir up old memories, and if so, let the memories rest. Write about why these people should have no place in your future.

_____

_____

_____

_____

SEVEN OF CUPS

STAY FOCUSED

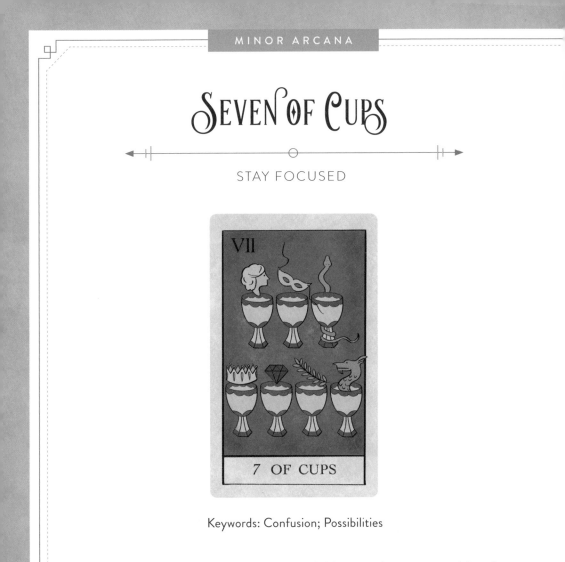

Keywords: Confusion; Possibilities

While the Seven of Cups brings the potential for amazing opportunities, these offers are insubstantial. It's not clear what's feasible and what's fantasy, as everything feels up in the air. Be discerning and find out what you can about each possible path, but ultimately you'll need to choose by paying attention to your instincts and emotions. This is not a test of logic; trust your inner knowing. This Seven is also the card of the visionary and shows the beginning stages of a new project, when anything is possible, as well as new doorways opening again as finances improve.

What feelings does this card evoke in you?

_____

_____

_____

_____

What's a recent decision you found difficult to make, and why was it so hard?

_____

_____

_____

_____

What are some things you do to procrastinate decision making (e.g., daydreaming, avoidance)?

_____

_____

_____

_____

Reversal: The reversed Seven has much the same meaning as the upright card, but here, extreme emotions are in play. Be aware of the danger of idealizing a situation and avoiding a difficult truth; in relationships, the card can mean being deceived by appearances. This is not the right time for commitment; avoid becoming embroiled in drama.

_____

_____

_____

_____

EIGHT OF CUPS

CHANGE THINGS UP

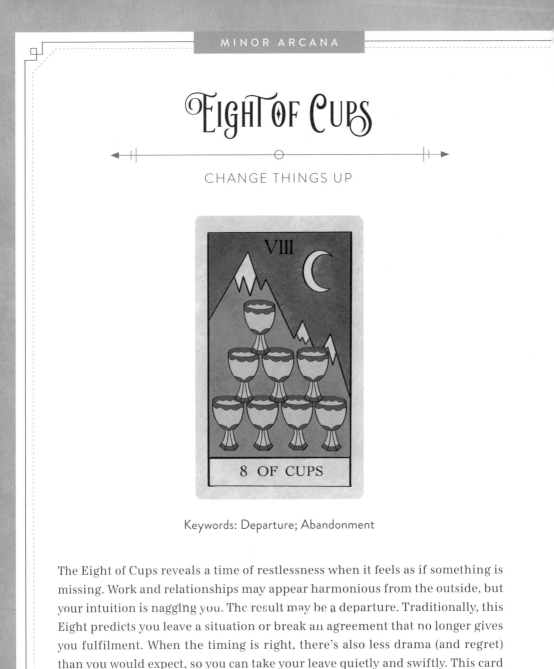

Keywords: Departure; Abandonment

The Eight of Cups reveals a time of restlessness when it feels as if something is missing. Work and relationships may appear harmonious from the outside, but your intuition is nagging you. The result may be a departure. Traditionally, this Eight predicts you leave a situation or break an agreement that no longer gives you fulfilment. When the timing is right, there's also less drama (and regret) than you would expect, so you can take your leave quietly and swiftly. This card often shows that you have already left a situation emotionally, so now take your actual leave.

What feelings does this card evoke in you?

_____

_____

_____

_____

Is there something or someone you've left behind (or should leave behind) so that you can
be more true to yourself?

_____

_____

_____

_____

Is there something missing in your life right now? How can you go about getting it?

_____

_____

_____

_____

Reversal: The Eight reversed shows errors of judgment, so you jump too soon or stay too
long, unable to see that there's an alternative way to do things. At this point, there's no
logical solution, so the way ahead is to follow your instincts. Timing is important, so trust
yourself that you will know the right time to move on.

_____

_____

_____

_____

Nine of Cups

APPRECIATE THE JOYS OF THE PRESENT

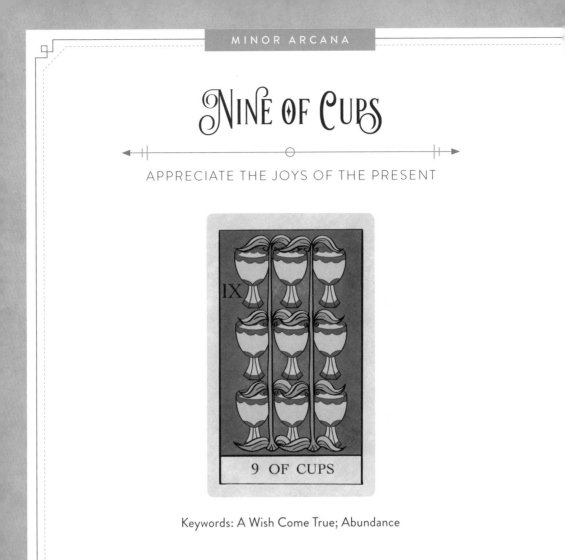

Keywords: A Wish Come True; Abundance

The Nine of Cups is known as the wish card because it foretells a dream come true. Joy comes from prosperity, generosity, and optimism, alongside parties and entertainment. This Nine reveals new romance and rewarding friendships. When fully living your truth, others respond. If you are nurturing a new project or idea, the card heralds its growth, so listen to your intuition, make time for the activities that make you happy, and see them flourish. This Nine also favors good health, as old tensions dissolve, flowing away in the waters of the past.

What feelings does this card evoke in you?

_____

_____

_____

_____

What's the one thing you would wish for right now? Is there anything you could do to help make it happen?

_____

_____

_____

_____

What are some activities that inspire joy? How can you fit them in more regularly?

_____

_____

_____

_____

Reversal: When the Nine is reversed, ego, self-centeredness, and emotional disconnection step in. This can manifest as smugness or narcissism. In personal and business projects, uncertainty rules due to misunderstandings; plans may be delayed and creativity can suffer. How can you focus on maintaining balance and routine? In what way can you take extra care of yourself?

_____

_____

_____

_____

TEN OF CUPS

THINK ABOUT WHAT TRULY MATTERS

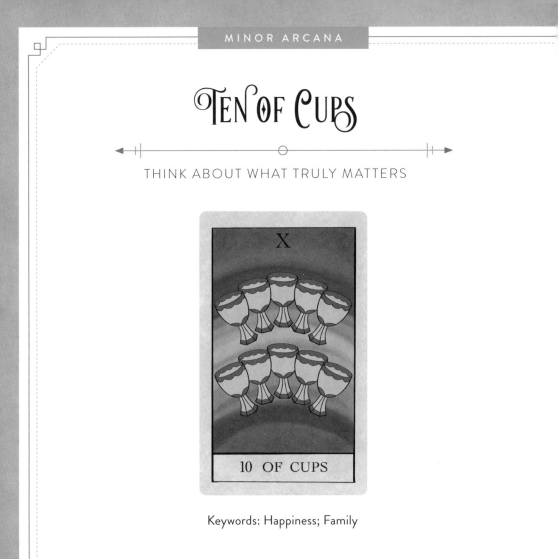

Keywords: Happiness; Family

One of the most positive cards, the Ten of Cups reveals the benefits of love and the security of family; it predicts great happiness for couples, families, and close friendships. Communication between family members will grow stronger and be more fulfilling. This Ten shows peace and harmony for business partnerships and other key networks. If you've been searching for a new home, it shows you will find the right property. In projects, the card gives assurance that what you have worked hard for will finally come together; this Ten is a wonderful indicator of prosperity.

What feelings does this card evoke in you?

_____

_____

_____

_____

Think of a time when you were content with your life. Was it because you had everything you wanted, or was it one thing in particular?

_____

_____

_____

_____

You might not have everything you want, but do you have everything you need?

_____

_____

_____

_____

Reversal: The reversed Ten retains much of its positive vibe, but with some irritating undercurrents and changes in friendships and family bonds. A family issue may need to be addressed as your routine is disrupted, or you sense discord in some relationships. Your plans to bring people together may falter due to miscommunication. Have you noticed any of this going on lately?

_____

_____

_____

_____

PAGE OF CUPS

ENJOY LiFE'S PLEASURES

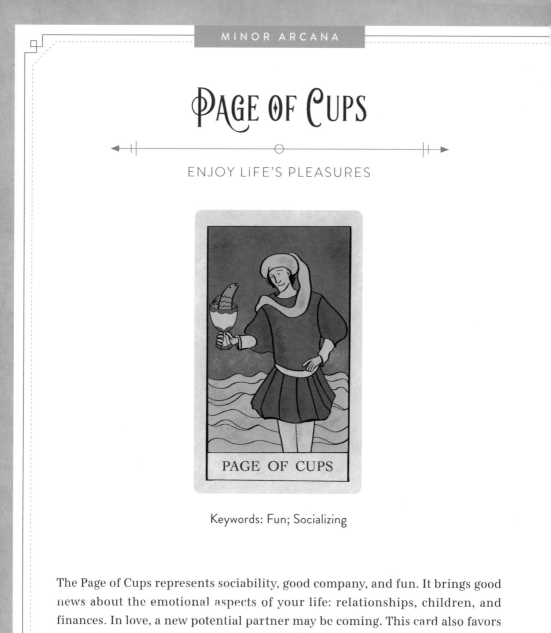

PAGE OF CUPS

Keywords: Fun; Socializing

The Page of Cups represents sociability, good company, and fun. It brings good news about the emotional aspects of your life: relationships, children, and finances. In love, a new potential partner may be coming. This card also favors imagination and creativity, and so bodes well for new projects and opportunities to improve your home and lifestyle. If you've suffered periods of insecurity and doubt, this Page assures you that all is well, and good times are ahead. Finances are also favored now.

What feelings does this card evoke in you?

_____

_____

_____

_____

Are you a sociable person, and what do you enjoy about spending time with others?

_____

_____

_____

_____

Write about a new project or opportunity that's on your horizon where you can flex your creativity and imagination.

_____

_____

_____

_____

Reversal: The reversed Page brings frustration and irresponsibility. Offers do not materialize; you may feel that life is all work and no play. As a person, the reversed Page is emotionally immature and attention-seeking, so you cannot rely on their perspective. Are you feeling like you're all work and no play right now, or spinning your wheels with nothing to show for it?

_____

_____

_____

_____

Knight of Cups

FALL HEAD OVER HEELS (WITH CARE)

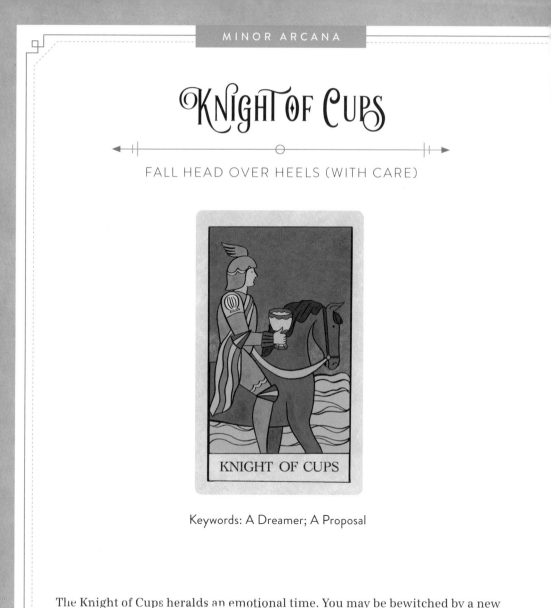

Keywords: A Dreamer; A Proposal

The Knight of Cups heralds an emotional time. You may be bewitched by a new love interest (or several), you may enjoy more romance with an existing partner, or new friends may enter your circle. But tread carefully, as this Knight is an idealist and, while wanting a relationship, finds it hard to articulate their true feelings. They may be stuck behind a persona of the perfect partner but unable to drop the act to let you see who they really are.

What feelings does this card evoke in you?

_____

_____

_____

_____

Are you open to having a new love or friend in your life right now? How would you show them that they're cared for?

_____

_____

_____

Are you about to take a trip with someone important to you? If not, write about where you would like to go, even if it's just a day trip.

_____

_____

_____

Reversal: The reversed Knight means disappointment; an offer that at first glance appeared perfect does not materialize. As a person, the reversed Knight is untrustworthy and unreliable, perhaps a lover who has intimacy and commitment issues. It is of course best for you to step away, as this Knight has little to offer other than ongoing drama. Is there drama in your life right now, and how can you best get away from it?

_____

_____

_____

_____

QUEEN OF CUPS

FOLLOW YOUR HEART

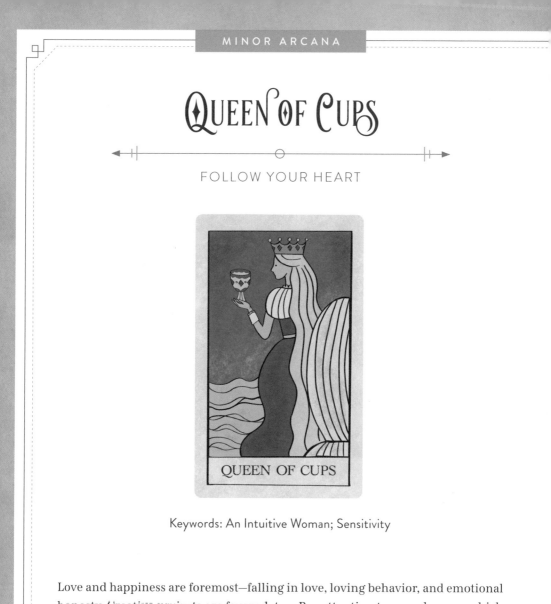

QUEEN OF CUPS

Keywords: An Intuitive Woman; Sensitivity

Love and happiness are foremost—falling in love, loving behavior, and emotional honesty. Creative projects are favored, too. Pay attention to your dreams, which hold messages for you. The Queen of Cups predicts the positive influence of an intuitive, sensitive woman. She is nurturing and compassionate, with high emotional intelligence. This card often comes up in readings to show the ideal female partner, who is unafraid of intimacy while having stability and appropriate boundaries. This Queen can predict motherhood and children, too.

What feelings does this card evoke in you?

_____

_____

_____

_____

Can you tell what others need before they do?

_____

_____

_____

_____

Write about someone in your life who is a good listener and is compassionate to you.

_____

_____

_____

_____

Reversal: The reversed Queen suggests you suffer emotional or financial pressure. There may be jealousy in a relationship, or maybe unfaithfulness. The Queen has obsessive tendencies, competes for attention, and needs to have her own way at all times. She drains those around her. Can you think of someone like this? What are some way that you can not facilitate her needs or not commit to her?

_____

_____

_____

_____

KING OF CUPS

RISE ABOVE NEGATIVITY

Keywords: A Warmhearted Man; Support

Use your heart and intuition to settle a conflict that arises, either within yourself or between you and others, usually in a work or family situation. In negotiations, use all your charm and empathy. When others feel that you are really engaged with them, they will drop their defenses and communication will improve.

What feelings does this card evoke in you?

_____

_____

_____

_____

Are you in a relationship or situation that's emotionally draining, and what can you do to step away from it?

_____

_____

_____

_____

Write about someone in your life whom you can turn to for support, either now or in the past.

_____

_____

_____

_____

Reversal: The reversed King reveals emotional vulnerability. You may be dealing with someone who is volatile right now, perhaps with destructive behavioral patterns or addiction issues; they may be secretive, ashamed, and uncommunicative when not blaming others for their predicament. Does this describe someone in your life, either now or in the past?

_____

_____

_____

Ace of Pentacles

HAVE WHAT YOU DESIRE

Keywords: Money; Success; Beginnings

The Ace of Pentacles is auspicious for every aspect of your life. It predicts happiness and contentment, as well as prosperity and the way to achieve it. In readings, it commonly arises to show money is coming, or a new property; it also predicts foundation and stability, so if you have questions concerning your home or relationship, you will receive what you need in abundance. Do not doubt your good fortune. You deserve it.

What feelings does this card evoke in you?

_____

_____

_____

_____

What you would do if a little cash came your way, say $50? What about $500? $5000?

_____

_____

_____

_____

A new opportunity has presented itself and might be your chance to achieve what you've been striving for. How do you seize the moment? Are you willing to do what needs to be done?

_____

_____

_____

_____

Reversal: The reversed Ace reveals greed and holding fast to one outcome. Desperation can cause materialistic thinking. The card also shows financial mismanagement and mistakes. In relationships, someone close becomes grasping and materialistic, wanting to keep everything for themselves. The card can also show gambling and reckless spending. Is there a financial decision you need to make? Write out some pros and cons before making a decision.

_____

_____

_____

_____

Two of Pentacles

BE MINDFUL OF MONEY

Keywords: Decisions; Balance

The Two of Pentacles shows making a decision and, in particular, managing money. There may be temporary cash-flow issues, and you'll need consistent effort to balance the books. On a more positive note, the card says that if you pay close attention to financial and property matters, you will manage well, even on a tight budget. This Two indicates fairness and a willingness to find a good balance between work and personal life. The card often comes up to show two properties and, sometimes, making a decision about where to live.

What feelings does this card evoke in you?

_____

_____

_____

_____

What are some ways that you cope with difficulties?

_____

_____

_____

_____

You have a lot going on. How are you balancing your priorities—are you a good enough juggler, or is it time to cut back?

_____

_____

_____

_____

Reversal: The reversed Two shows egotism and pride get in the way of practicality. Irresponsible spending and a generally reckless attitude toward money may cause hardship. In work, you may be dealing with an unreasonable boss who is unrealistic about what can be achieved. The card can also show the ending of a business partnership due to financial difficulties. Are you experiencing needless pressure at work or financial troubles with another person?

_____

_____

_____

_____

Three of Pentacles

GIVE YOURSELF A PAT ON THE BACK

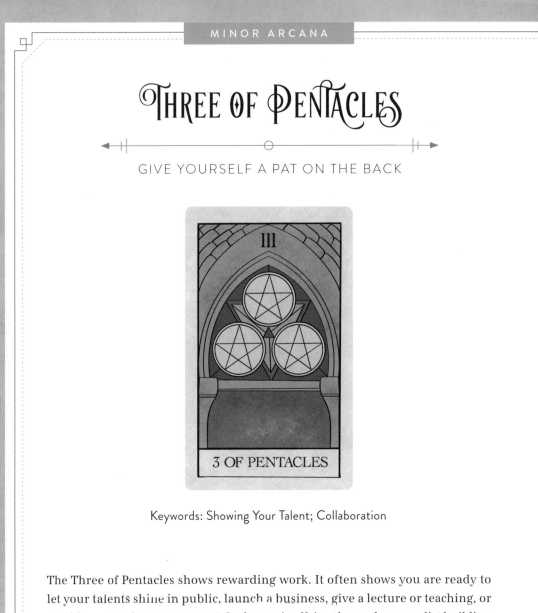

Keywords: Showing Your Talent; Collaboration

The Three of Pentacles shows rewarding work. It often shows you are ready to let your talents shine in public, launch a business, give a lecture or teaching, or preside over an important event. In domestic affairs, the card can predict building or improvement work to your home or putting a property up for sale. This Three is also a good card for creatives, predicting that projects will be finished and appreciated. The downside as you succeed is the touch of envy you may sense around you; this jealousy is transitory and will not harm your progress.

What feelings does this card evoke in you?

_____

_____

_____

_____

How do you feel about having success? Did you earn it by pulling you own weight? Are you concerned about how others might see you now?

_____

_____

_____

_____

You have talents, but you didn't secure everything you have on your own. Write about who has helped you along the way.

_____

_____

_____

_____

Reversal: The versed Three indicates work is tiresome, and you may not be willing to put in the groundwork. This may be because you've become cynical about finding a career that will suit. You'll need to push through the dull details or make a swift decision to move on. Another interpretation of the card is poor planning, causing a project to not succeed. Write about where you see your career going and what you need to do to make it happen.

_____

_____

_____

_____

FOUR OF PENTACLES

PROTECT YOUR ASSETS

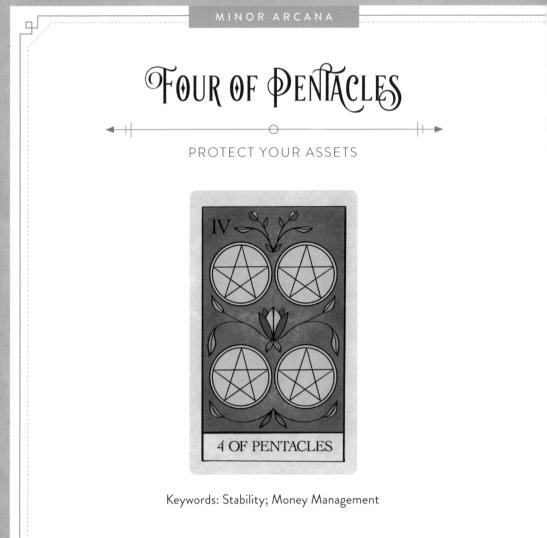

Keywords: Stability; Money Management

The Four of Pentacles shows the need for stability and establishing a firm foundation. If you have suffered past hardship, the tough times are over, as now your work pays off. While this doesn't indicate a huge windfall, you will have enough money and acknowledgment to feel satisfied. The card also shows protection of assets and traditional values. In work, you attain a position that is very secure. An additional meaning of this Four is the miser, but this money has come from hard work. You'll value what you have achieved and, for now, want to keep it for yourself.

What feelings does this card evoke in you?

_____

_____

_____

_____

Think about a time when money was tight. Does that inform how you spend money now?

_____

_____

_____

_____

When money comes in, do you set some aside for savings? Is there a difference in the things you should be saving for versus what you _want_ to save for?

_____

_____

_____

Reversal: The reversed Four reveals an overly materialistic individual who holds too fast to status and possessions. Try to let go of insecurity, as this can feed a belief that you'll never have enough. In work, the card can reveal that you miss opportunities because your confidence is low. It can also suggest a person who is showy or smug; in a position of power over you, you may find this individual controlling and self-centered. Write about some things you feel you don't have, or about a person you feel is obnoxious about what they have.

_____

_____

_____

_____

Five of Pentacles

HELP YOURSELF

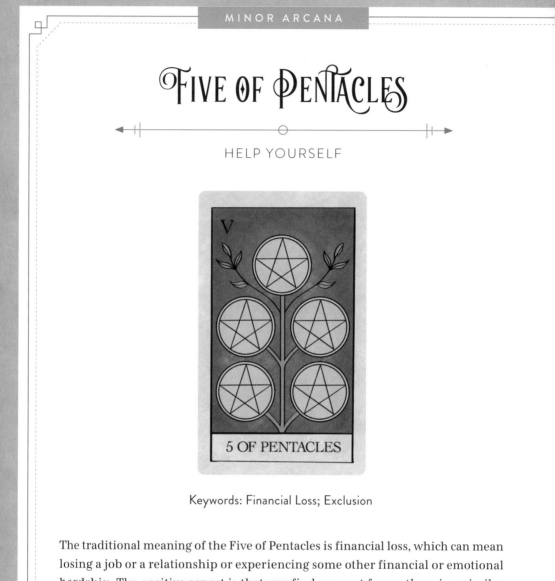

Keywords: Financial Loss; Exclusion

The traditional meaning of the Five of Pentacles is financial loss, which can mean losing a job or a relationship or experiencing some other financial or emotional hardship. The positive aspect is that you find support from others in a similar position. Consider new options, and you may discover another resource or approach that will help you see a way forward. This Five often shows a fear of poverty and isolation, rather than actual poverty. It also commonly shows a fear of losing the security of home and/or the aftermath of a relationship breakup, with one partner feeling alone and depleted.

What feelings does this card evoke in you?

_____

_____

_____

_____

Think of a time where you struggled and write about how you overcame it.

_____

_____

_____

_____

When you hit a bad patch, remind yourself that help can usually be found. You just need to look around you. Who in your life can you turn to?

_____

_____

_____

_____

Reversal: The reversed Five asks you to examine your values. Fear of change could lead you to ignore debt or become oblivious to growing tensions. Hoarding old possessions and memories shows you need to feel safe and don't have the faith that you'll be supported in the future. In relationships, you may suffer due to a partner's selfish behavior. If you're clinging to objects, people, or money, what are you avoiding?

_____

_____

_____

_____

SIX OF PENTACLES

SHARE THE WEALTH

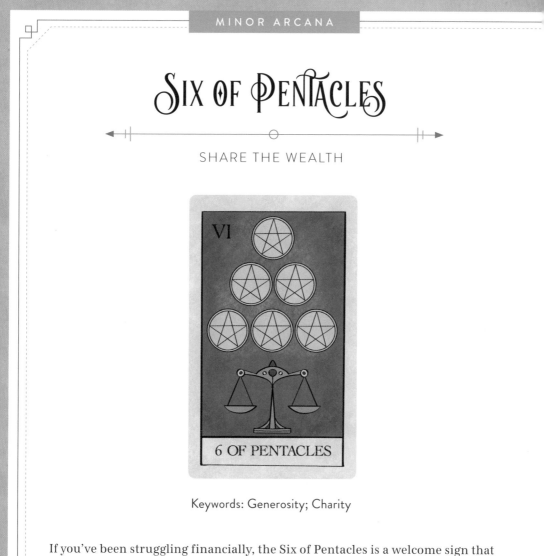

Keywords: Generosity; Charity

If you've been struggling financially, the Six of Pentacles is a welcome sign that your circumstances will certainly improve. Equally, the card can show that you are the benefactor, so you may help a friend with a temporary cash-flow problem, or you feel drawn to support a charity that is close to your heart. Any money that may be coming to you will allow you to pay off any outstanding debt and/or invest the money wisely in your future. Overall, this Six brings genuine support and predicts you feeling connected and close to your usual circle of friends and family.

What feelings does this card evoke in you?

_____

_____

_____

_____

Write about what you would do with a change in financial circumstances, such as getting a better-paying job or paying off your car or student loan. What would you do with that "extra" money?

_____

_____

_____

_____

Have you come into some good fortune? Nothing shows your appreciation for everything you have been given like giving to others. How can you spread the wealth?

_____

_____

_____

Reversal: The reversed Six shows money coming to you but you cannot keep it—usually due to carelessness or theft. Guard your possessions carefully and watch what you spend. The card also suggests there may be envy due to money, so monitor your attitude and the attitudes of people around you. What are some ways that you "carelessly" spend money?

_____

_____

_____

_____

Seven of Pentacles

KEEP GOING—YOU'RE NEARLY THERE!

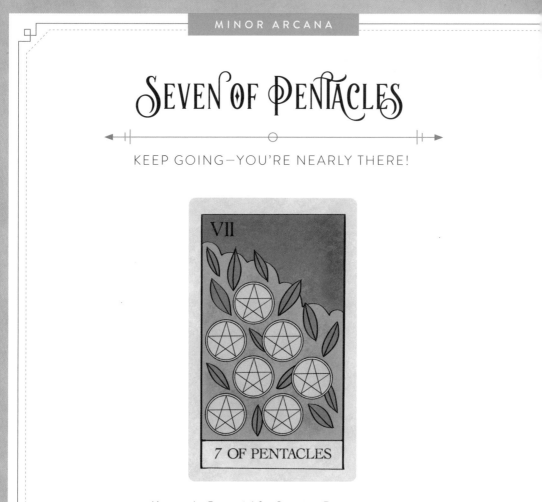

Keywords: Potential for Success; Perseverance

There's a goal in sight, and you are close to achieving it—but now is not the time to stop and reflect. The Seven of Pentacles is the card of doing, not philosophizing, so keep your focus on what you want and believe you can achieve it. The card often shows the need to keep your career goals in sight or to work through a tedious stage in a tiresome project; it can also show saving for a home or expanding a business. In domestic affairs, this Seven can show there's no money left for little luxuries.

What feelings does this card evoke in you?

_____

_____

_____

_____

When you're close to being done with something, do you find you run out of patience, or do you still keep working hard, knowing the end is in sight?

_____

_____

_____

_____

Write about some goals you have, both short-term and long-term.

_____

_____

_____

_____

Reversal: The reversed Seven means procrastination. Commit fully to the work you're doing or the lifestyle you have, regardless of the ups and downs—or put your energies elsewhere. This may mean considering a different job or career path. But act now, as any decision is better than no decision at all. An additional meaning of the card is anxiety about a loan or other financial agreement. What is it that you're procrastinating about, and why do you think that is?

_____

_____

_____

_____

Eight of Pentacles

TAKE YOUR SKILLS ALL THE WAY TO THE BANK

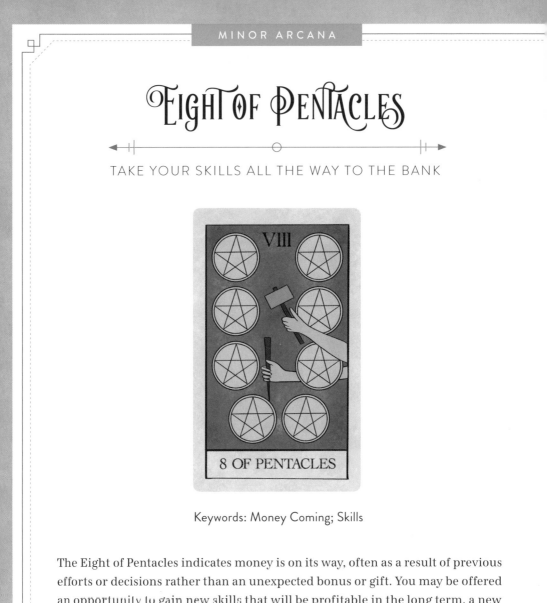

Keywords: Money Coming; Skills

The Eight of Pentacles indicates money is on its way, often as a result of previous efforts or decisions rather than an unexpected bonus or gift. You may be offered an opportunity to gain new skills that will be profitable in the long term, a new career direction, or a promotion. In general, this Eight also reflects the need for a logical, diligent approach to your projects. This card, often known as the apprentice, shows education, particularly an undergraduate degree or diploma. This Eight also reveals a hardworking, trustworthy, and dedicated individual who takes his or her responsibilities seriously.

What feelings does this card evoke in you?

_____

_____

_____

_____

Think about a skill, talent, or degree you have that took a long time to obtain. Write about what helped you stay the course and commit until the end.

_____

_____

_____

_____

Think about a skill, talent, or degree you would like to have. Write about some things that you will need to do accomplish it.

_____

_____

_____

Reversal: The reversed Eight can show that you're feeling trapped, maybe because you've chosen an educational course that isn't for you. In work, you may know you're only doing the job for the money, which may be acceptable in the short-term basis, but long-term feels soul-destroying. It may be time to look elsewhere. Don't resign yourself to your present situation if there's no sense of achievement or appreciation. Does this speak to you?

_____

_____

_____

_____

NINE OF PENTACLES

TREAT YOURSELF!

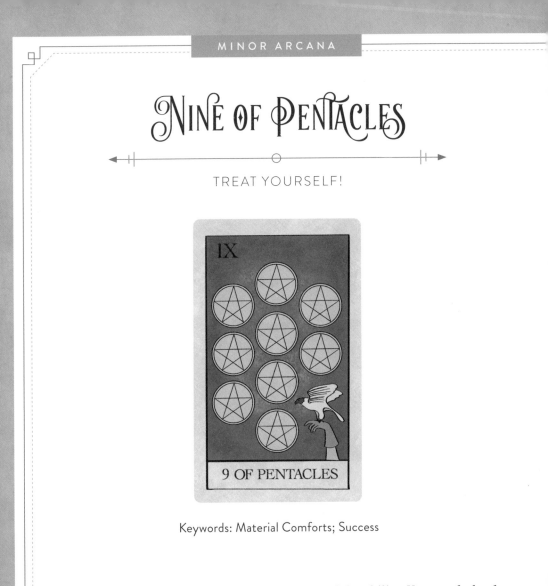

Keywords: Material Comforts; Success

The Nine of Pentacles ushers in a time of financial stability. You can feel safe in your home, surround yourself with objects you love, and be proud of your achievements. It's time to appreciate all that you have, so leisure time beckons; enjoy the fruits of your work. You can focus on your own needs without feeling guilty. This Nine also brings a sense of serenity and relaxation, so it predicts you can feel at home, and at one, with yourself. In work matters, it can predict financial reward for your efforts.

What feelings does this card evoke in you?

_____

_____

_____

_____

What are some creature comforts you've earned that you're proud of?

_____

_____

_____

_____

Prosperity and achievement might be in your grasp; you have something to celebrate. Are you solitary in this state or is that independence? Explore in writing.

_____

_____

_____

_____

Reversal: The reversed Nine can show vanity and ego at large; the urge for material wealth gets out of control. In general, the card can show financial dependence that is uncomfortable or misuse of money for selfish means. An additional meaning is feeling that your home is somehow under threat because you are struggling with debt. Don't struggle alone—write about where you can turn for help.

_____

_____

_____

_____

TEN OF PENTACLES

GROW STRONG LIKE AN OAK

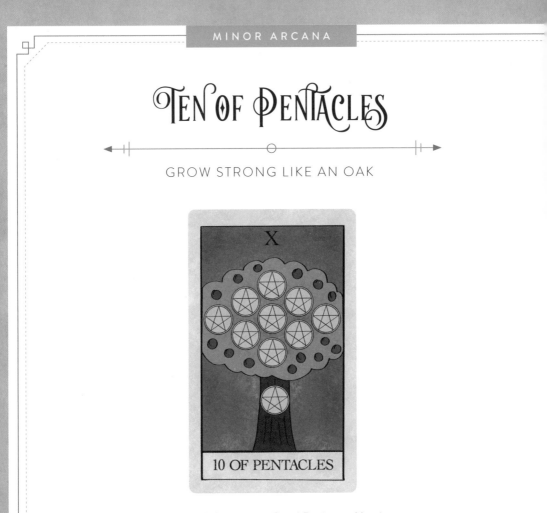

Keywords: Inheritance; Good Business; Marriage

The Ten of Pentacles shows an inheritance, generosity, and a love relationship that brings wealth and happiness. It often shows a wedding. An additional meaning is inherited property, buying a second home, or extending your current home, again with family support. Note that family in this context signifies those you consider family and treat as such, so this could relate to a close circle of longtime friends. This Ten also suggests maturity in financial terms, with investments maturing, as well as in emotional terms, as the emotional maturity that comes with life experience.

What feelings does this card evoke in you?

_____

_____

_____

_____

What makes you feel safe and well supported, and does the answer change when money is not a factor?

_____

_____

_____

Good things will come; maybe they have already. It is time to look back at what you have done—what you have gained?

_____

_____

_____

Reversal: The reversed Ten reveals communication problems in families as one generation tries to dominate another. General attitudes toward finances may be at the heart of the problem. This card often shows parents who try to control their families with money. In romantic relationships, money, property issues, and the demands of family get in the way of love. Ambition takes over; personal life comes second. Is any of this happening in your life right now?

_____

_____

_____

_____

Page of Pentacles

BE PRACTICAL AND DILIGENT

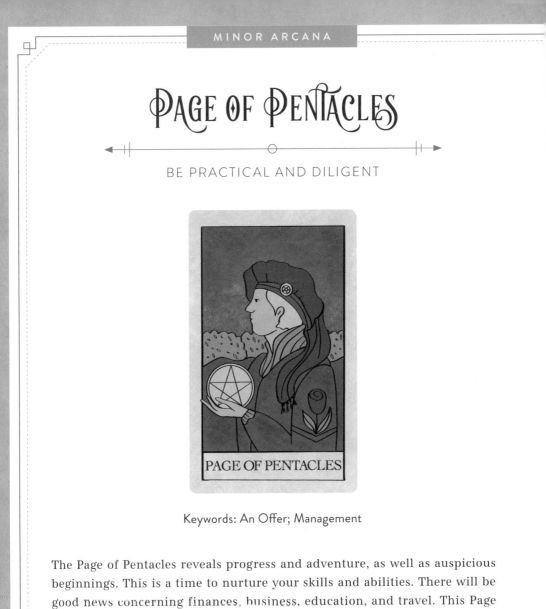

Keywords: An Offer; Management

The Page of Pentacles reveals progress and adventure, as well as auspicious beginnings. This is a time to nurture your skills and abilities. There will be good news concerning finances, business, education, and travel. This Page also highlights the need for management, and in work matters, there may be an opportunity to manage people and projects. There may be a job offer or an offer made on a property. Beware, as there is a real need for attention to detail now, and for diligence in all practical affairs. Double-check all arrangements and agreements.

What feelings does this card evoke in you?

_____

_____

_____

_____

What are some skills or abilities you could nurture at this time? Is there a way they can relate to finances or your work?

_____

_____

_____

_____

There is much for you to learn, and contemplation is your solace. While some might think you're dreaming, you're planning and growing. Where do you see yourself going?

_____

_____

_____

_____

Reversal: The reversed Page may be unwelcome news regarding finances or property. The card means extravagance and irresponsibility rule, and you may suffer due to someone else's selfish actions. The card can also apply to a person with a sense of entitlement who helps himself to what is yours; take some notes here for future reference.

_____

_____

_____

_____

KNIGHT OF PENTACLES

BE YOUR OWN BEST INVESTMENT

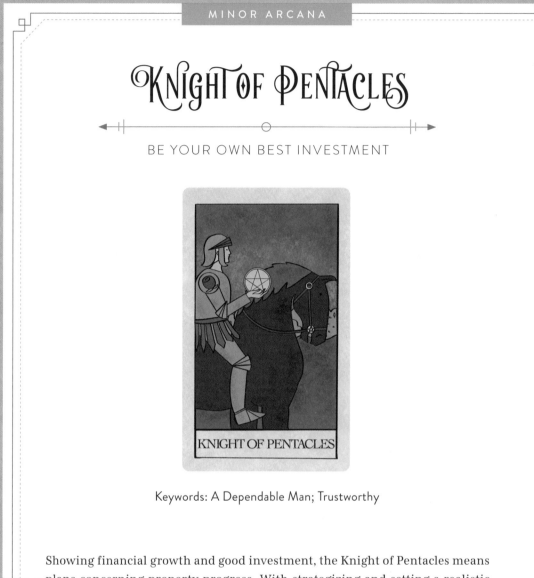

Keywords: A Dependable Man; Trustworthy

Showing financial growth and good investment, the Knight of Pentacles means plans concerning property progress. With strategizing and setting a realistic goal, you will succeed. Pay attention to the practical details now, and future benefits are assured. Get through boring and routine (but essential) tasks. In work, the card can indicate more money coming to you due to a raise, bonus, or promotion, but you may need to work harder in return. An additional meaning of this Knight is finding a secure home, potentially with a partner.

What feelings does this card evoke in you?

_____

_____

_____

_____

If you're a spender, what can you do to start curtailing your habits, and if you're a saver, is there more to investing that you could be doing?

_____

_____

_____

_____

Do you tend to pull "yourself up by your bootstraps" and get on with the task at hand? If not, what holds you back?

_____

_____

_____

_____

Reversal: The reversed Knight advises that you avoid complacency and check out all financial arrangements. The most negative interpretation of the card is financial mismanagement and misleading advice. Do you tend to "dot all I's and cross all T's" when it comes to finances?

_____

_____

_____

_____

QUEEN OF PENTACLES

BE THE QUEEN OF SELF-CARE

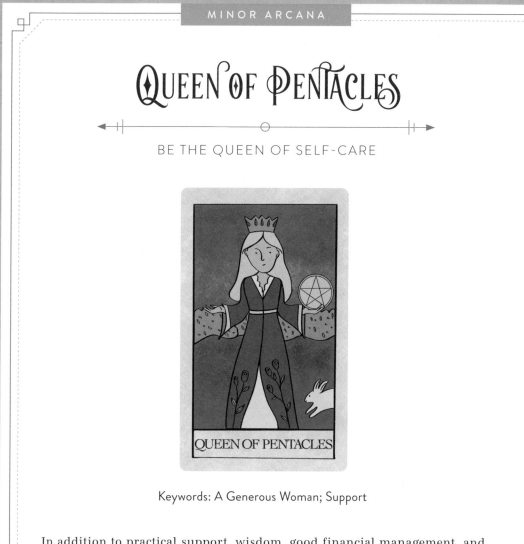

Keywords: A Generous Woman; Support

In addition to practical support, wisdom, good financial management, and financial help, the Queen of Pentacles can show marriage and money coming to a couple. It is also a card for good health, a sensual sex life, and fertility. This Queen is well-off, generous, and supportive. She likes the good things in life and knows how to spend money—on beautiful objects, on gifts for loved ones, and on herself. She's physically affectionate and hands-on in her projects; she'll lend practical help. She commonly shows up as a benefactor and reminds you to care for your body and your finances.

What feelings does this card evoke in you?

_____

_____

_____

_____

How important are material possessions to you, and do you feel better when buying them, or when you can look at them or use them every day?

_____

_____

_____

_____

Nurturing is hard work! Are you taking care of others or are you too busy taking care of yourself? Do things need rebalancing?

_____

_____

_____

_____

Reversal: When the Queen is reversed, finances can suffer. Money you relied upon doesn't roll in, or funds are misappropriated. You may have to deal with the impact of someone's financial mishaps, but this is temporary. An additional meaning is your home is neglected while other concerns take over. Are you neglecting some things right now while your mind is consumed with others?

_____

_____

_____

_____

King of Pentacles

MAKE THE MOST OF YOUR ASSETS

Keywords: A Prosperous Man; Security

Financial and property matters improve, and you enjoy success and comfort. The King of Pentacles also predicts conflicts that will be resolved. In relationships, he offers security and loyalty. A visionary man with a plan, this King will work hard for rewards and is usually well-off. He is reliable and generous and offers practical support. Security is important to him, and he is happiest in a settled relationship. He needs to be a protector, and he has firm boundaries—he will not tolerate those looking to take what is his.

What feelings does this card evoke in you?

_____

_____

_____

_____

Think about how you handle finances. Could you enlist the help of someone, such as a financial planner, for advice? What would you ask them?

_____

_____

_____

_____

Sometimes your hard work can have a reward, whether that's a material thing or something as simple (but as needed) as some space to relax. Write about some ways that you can enjoy what you have earned.

_____

_____

_____

_____

Reversal: The reversed King is greedy and untrustworthy, so double-check all financial agreements to ensure that there are no hidden catches. Debt is an interpretation of the reversed King, so turn the spotlight on your finances now to limit the damage of overspending. Write about where you might be overspending.

_____

_____

_____

_____

ACE OF SWORDS

HIT THAT BULL'S-EYE

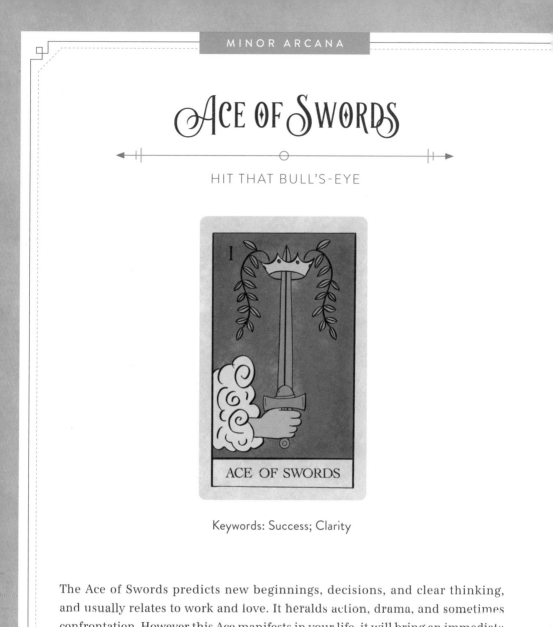

Keywords: Success; Clarity

The Ace of Swords predicts new beginnings, decisions, and clear thinking, and usually relates to work and love. It heralds action, drama, and sometimes confrontation. However this Ace manifests in your life, it will bring an immediate change to your circumstances—for the better. Mental agility and assertiveness will bring success. Do not be overzealous; judge the situation and be direct rather than abrasive. In relationships, this Ace reveals triumph over past obstacles—you win through to your heart's desire.

What feelings does this card evoke in you?

_____

_____

_____

_____

Is your mind an incubator of ideas? Write about a time when something small turned into a big (positive) change in your life.

_____

_____

_____

You could have just had, or be on the verge of, a significant breakthrough that may be a change in your circumstances or a new understanding of the world. Write about what this might be or mean for you.

_____

_____

_____

Reversal: The reversed Ace can predict conflict and arguments, and you may become involved in a hurtful battle of wills. The card can also predict a contest that you cannot win, at least at present. The message is to withdraw, tend your wounds, and turn your attentions elsewhere. Is there a no-win conflict you're currently battling, and if so, how can you withdraw?

_____

_____

_____

_____

TWO OF SWORDS

PLAN FOR BATTLE

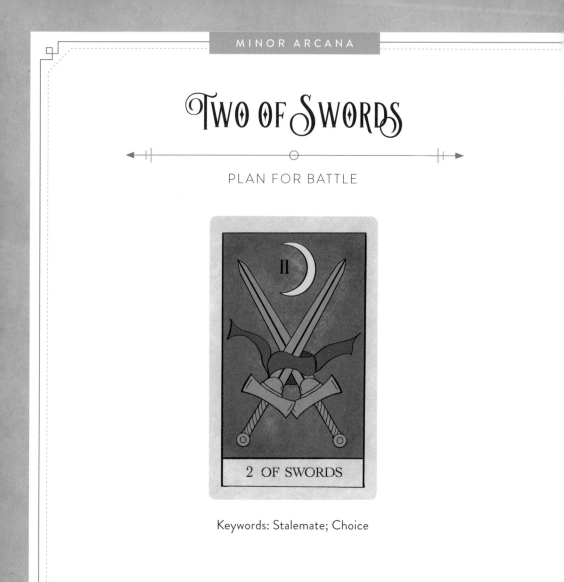

Keywords: Stalemate; Choice

The Two of Swords shows thinking time before a decision. A situation has reached a stalemate, so view this period as a truce before further negotiation. Protect yourself, have some peace, and don't take action. The upcoming battle may not go away; resolve it now and it's done, or the situation will fester and may return. Two swords on the card can reveal a person you "cross swords with," but stand your ground and say what you think. Help is at hand in the form of supportive friends and colleagues. Listen to advice, then take the best practical steps forward.

What feelings does this card evoke in you?

_____

_____

_____

_____

Are you facing a decision that involves other people? Write about what's important to you and what you think is important to them; maybe you'll find some common ground—and a way forward.

_____

_____

_____

There are important choices to make about your future, but the way ahead is unclear and you may feel stuck. You have all the tools you need to make your decision—what might they be?

_____

_____

_____

Reversal: The traditional meaning of the reversed Two is deception and being blind to someone's manipulation. This card applies particularly to partnerships—love, friendships, business, and your career. If your intuition is telling you that someone is dishonest, pay attention. There's an opportunity here to act, but don't delay. Take a look at a relationship where you're feeling uneasy and really consider if you're being manipulated; write about it here.

_____

_____

_____

Three of Swords

GET TO THE HEART OF THE MATTER

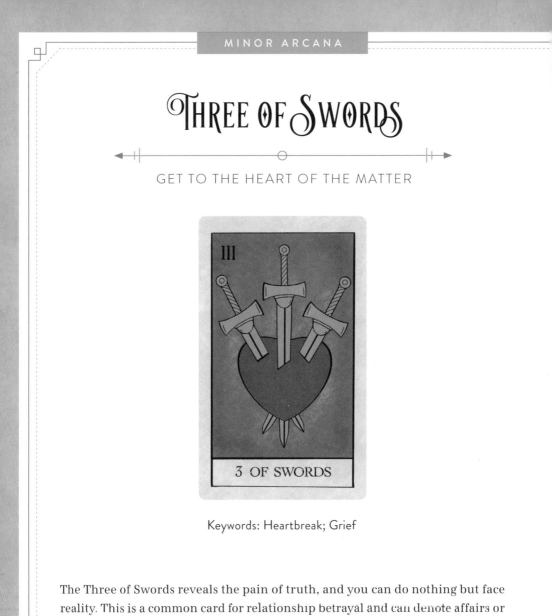

Keywords: Heartbreak; Grief

The Three of Swords reveals the pain of truth, and you can do nothing but face reality. This is a common card for relationship betrayal and can denote affairs or disloyalty in other life areas, such as work relationships and business dealings. On a more positive note, any confusion is banished, and you can now recover from shock, begin the healing process, and move forward. In health, this Three can relate to heart issues that may need attention. (This is a message to take care of the heart and safeguard health; it is not a prediction of serious illness.)

What feelings does this card evoke in you?

_____

_____

_____

_____

Think of an argument that hurt you, or maybe even ended a relationship. Have you been able to forgive or heal? Write what you would say to that person now, if you could.

_____

_____

_____

Loss and pain are unavoidable, but they're not permanent. Facing your hurt can bring it down to size and maybe even make the next time easier to bear. Write about a specific heartache here.

_____

_____

_____

Reversal: When the Three reverses, the upset of the upright card is accompanied by quarrels and drama. In a sense, despite the upheaval, this gives a more positive meaning than that of the upright card, as at least feelings are expressed, and some of the confusion and pain is shared and released. Those around you will understand your need to vent, but write some thoughts here.

_____

_____

_____

_____

Four of Swords

TAKE A TIME-OUT

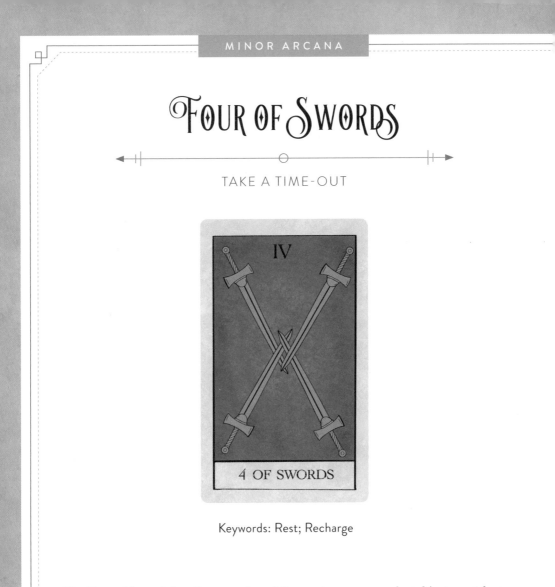

Keywords: Rest; Recharge

The Four of Swords has the meaning of time out, so you may be taking a rest from work, a personal project, or a relationship. The card often comes up in readings in the past or present position to show taking a break from a relationship and also the need for recovery from illness or an operation. Commonly, as a prediction card, this Four shows recovery from stress, so the message is to conserve your energy and take quiet time if you can. The card is a nudge to take some time alone to recharge.

What feelings does this card evoke in you?

_____

_____

_____

_____

Make a list of things that are worrying you or stressing you out. Then write about one thing you can try to lessen the worry or the stress for each item.

_____

_____

_____

_____

While a good defense can be a good offense, sometimes an even better defense is doing nothing at all. Pulling back from the world is a perfectly fine reaction to tough times. What are some things you can do to rest and recover so that when you return you are prepared?

_____

_____

_____

_____

Reversal: The reversed Four enforces the time-out message—so you may have to take time away from work or other responsibilities due to influences out of your control. This is a phase, so find peace and use the time positively. Write about how you may need to rethink your working arrangements or come to terms with changes in a relationship.

_____

_____

_____

_____

Five of Swords

KNOW WHEN TO FOLD 'EM

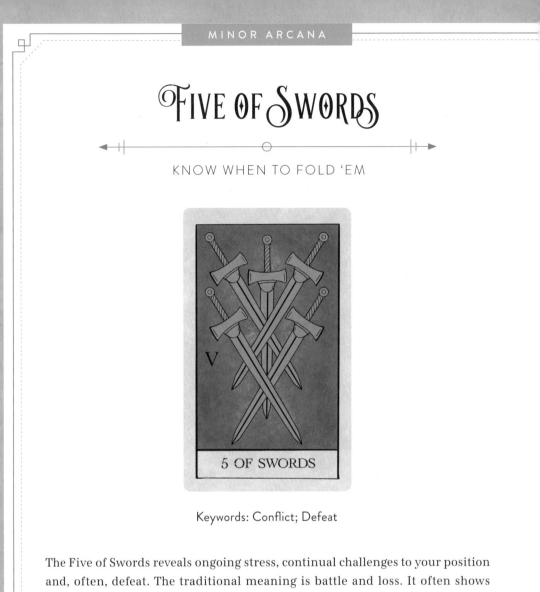

5 OF SWORDS

Keywords: Conflict; Defeat

The Five of Swords reveals ongoing stress, continual challenges to your position and, often, defeat. The traditional meaning is battle and loss. It often shows family disputes, conflicts with managers, and being a victim of "the system." In relationships, this Five predicts tension, but all is not lost. You may not win the battle, but you can recover and walk away with your self-respect—provided you make a gracious exit at the right time. There's a danger here that you'll continue the fight even when the battle is over. Regardless of the provocation, deal with your anger and disappointment. It's done.

What feelings does this card evoke in you?

_____

_____

_____

Think of a recent argument and write about your feelings. If you "won," did you hurt the other person's feelings? If you lost, could it have been better to walk away?

_____

_____

_____

Confidence is high in the aftermath of a victorious outcome, but it's easy to become cocky. Go ahead and gloat here to help get some of it out of your system.

_____

_____

_____

_____

Reversal: The reversed Five shows unnecessary conflict; you could become caught in the middle of another person's fight, and you may be the injured party through no fault of your own. Whoever initiates it has a selfish agenda, and the drama may be due to ego. The card suggests finding an opportunity to expose the unfairness, and to shift the balance of power. How does it feel to be caught in someone else's drama?

_____

_____

_____

_____

Six of Swords

STEP BACK FOR A SECOND

Keywords: Leaving Conflict Behind; Transition

The Six of Swords suggests moving on from a situation or relationship to enjoy a period of peace and harmony, whether that's physically or mentally, as you take a more detached approach. This opportunity to rest and recharge may lead you to explore a new environment or make a spiritual discovery. In work, this Six can show travel, and in relationships, it commonly shows two people spending time apart; more negatively, the interpretation is a relationship ending. On a more literal note, the card can simply show taking a break (and possible travel) from work or your usual environment.

What feelings does this card evoke in you?

_____

_____

_____

Is there a toxic person or situation in your life right now? Write about how you can take a mental break from them, and include some travel plans while you're at it.

_____

_____

_____

Transitions might be necessary, but they can often be difficult. The process of changing from one state of being or environment to another may cause friction, but you can also see it as a good time to let go of your past burdens. Face the future clearly, honestly, and positively, and write about it here.

_____

_____

_____

Reversal: The reversed Six has a meaning that is similar to that of the upright card. It reveals a need to escape, but your plans are delayed, as certain problems need to be resolved before you can be free. Check that your intentions are sound, and keep your plans realistic. You may feel frustrated now by lack of progress, but stay focused and grounded and your time will come. What are some things you need to address before you can move on?

_____

_____

_____

Seven of Swords

KEEP YOUR WITS ABOUT YOU

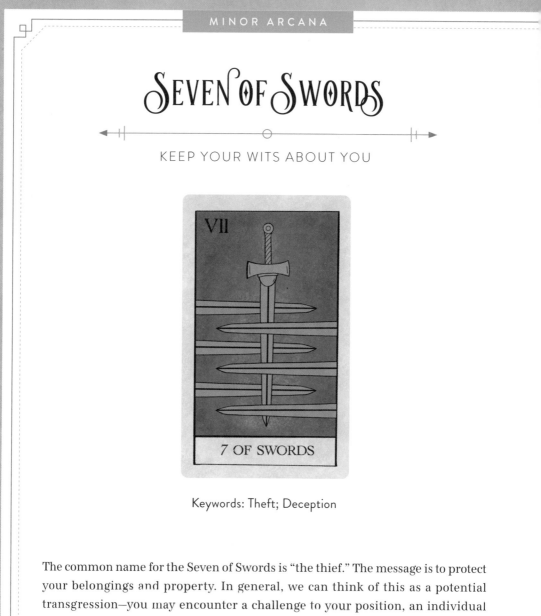

Keywords: Theft; Deception

The common name for the Seven of Swords is "the thief." The message is to protect your belongings and property. In general, we can think of this as a potential transgression—you may encounter a challenge to your position, an individual invading your space, or, in relationships, a selfish partner who takes too much emotionally, or, at worst, defrauds you. As the suit of Swords relates to intellect, you'll need your instincts and your wits to discover the truth. This Seven can also show legal problems, and unfair or fraudulent business dealings.

What feelings does this card evoke in you?

_____

_____

_____

Other than possessions, what else can be stolen? Do you feel less guilty (or less culpable)?

_____

_____

_____

_____

Honesty is always the best policy. Except when it's not. There are times when stealth is the better option. But not everybody is going to agree with that. Are there times when you were less than honest, told little white lies, or lied by omission—and what came afterwards?

_____

_____

_____

_____

Reversal: The reversed Seven shows a tendency to give up rather than take a stand. It may feel unnatural to you to think like your opponent to anticipate their next moves, but this attitude will help you defend what is yours. This particularly applies to work. The reversed Seven can show legal problems in business dealings, so beware of unscrupulous people. Who would you like to take a stand against, and if you could say anything you wanted to them, what would that be?

_____

_____

_____

Eight of Swords

BREAK THE BONDS

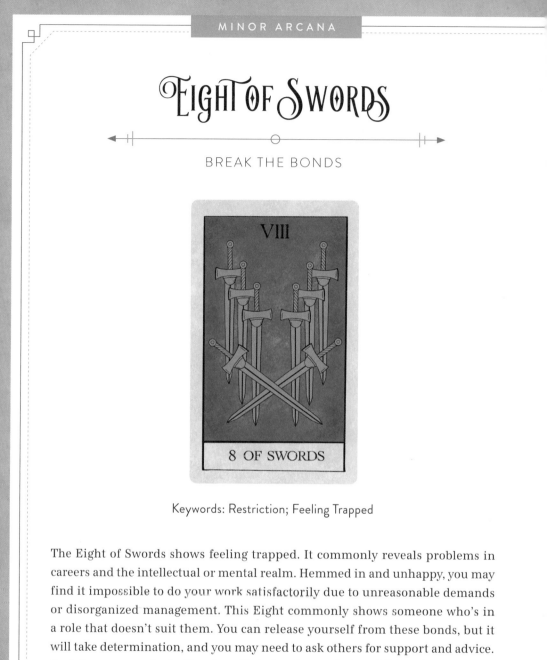

Keywords: Restriction; Feeling Trapped

The Eight of Swords shows feeling trapped. It commonly reveals problems in careers and the intellectual or mental realm. Hemmed in and unhappy, you may find it impossible to do your work satisfactorily due to unreasonable demands or disorganized management. This Eight commonly shows someone who's in a role that doesn't suit them. You can release yourself from these bonds, but it will take determination, and you may need to ask others for support and advice. Socially, you may be feeling humiliated or ignored. An additional meaning of the card is illness and incapacity, as a phase of physical restriction.

What feelings does this card evoke in you?

_____

_____

_____

_____

In what ways do you feel stuck, and where do you feel most cornered in your life?

_____

_____

_____

_____

Some traps we set ourselves, but the good news is that those can be the easier ones to deal with once we find them. What might be some of these personal traps you've set?

_____

_____

_____

_____

Reversal: The reversed Eight retains much of the upright meaning, except that it's often accompanied by guilt, anger, and regret. It's likely you'll express these feelings in negative ways because you're so frustrated; this phase won't last, so try not to lash out at whoever is closest, and write your feelings here.

_____

_____

_____

_____

NINE OF SWORDS

DON'T BE A WORRY-WART

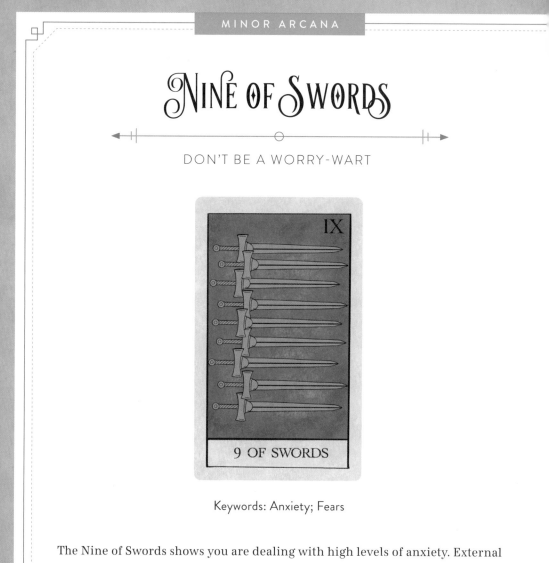

Keywords: Anxiety; Fears

The Nine of Swords shows you are dealing with high levels of anxiety. External events may have triggered the initial stress, but the issue now is how you are responding to it. The card also indicates the habit of worry—you may be worrying about inconsequential things that usually don't warrant your attention. Thankfully, as this is a minor card, this pattern is temporary. In work, this Nine can show feeling overwhelmed; you simply have too much to do. The card occasionally shows mental health issues associated with anxiety, such as panic disorder, depression, insomnia, and nightmares.

What feelings does this card evoke in you?

_____

_____

_____

_____

Is there one predominant worry in your life? Write to it now, telling it exactly how it makes you feel. (Giving it a name and a form might help.)

_____

_____

_____

_____

Your worry has no limit. Some things can be real, but others may be just anxieties or figments of your imagination. Separate the real from the imagined by writing about your worries here.

_____

_____

_____

Reversal: The reversed Nine's meaning is more extreme than that of its upright counterpart: despair, guilt, or feeling trapped. But this is the lowest point of the cycle, and these feelings will begin to shift. Be patient and compassionate with yourself and turn to others for support. Write some advice to yourself, but make it as tender and compassionate as if you were writing to a dear friend.

_____

_____

_____

_____

TEN OF SWORDS

LET IT GO

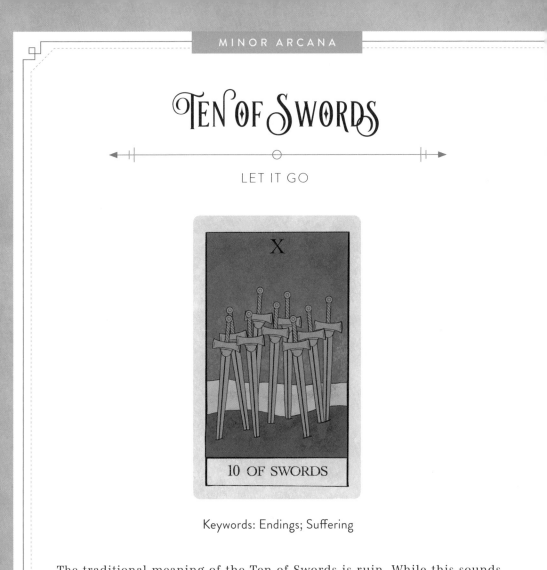

Keywords: Endings; Suffering

The traditional meaning of the Ten of Swords is ruin. While this sounds frightening, it doesn't mean death or destruction. This ending clears the way for new possibilities. In your personal life, bonds of friendship may break; you may see that certain people in a group were causing discord and stress. In love relationships, this Ten signifies a dramatic ending. In work, this may manifest as the closure of a department or a failing business. More positively, this is the end of an era; soon the strife and upset will be over. Health issues, such as low energy and exhaustion, will improve.

What feelings does this card evoke in you?

_____

_____

_____

_____

Is there someone in your life who has hit a low point? What are some ways you might be able to help them?

_____

_____

_____

_____

Things may look dark. When dealt a serious blow, it can be easy to lose hope, but you're still standing. Now is a time for rebuilding, so write out your plan here.

_____

_____

_____

_____

Reversal: The reversed Ten holds the meaning of the upright card but indicates there may be more repercussions. You may examine your past and feel guilty or angry and react more deeply to a fallout; try not to hold on to the stress, accept the situation, and let go. The card can also show feeling helpless. Write about a past hurt that still bothers you and with each word, commit to letting it go.

_____

_____

_____

_____

PAGE OF SWORDS

KEEP YOUR EARS OPEN

PAGE OF SWORDS

Keywords: Gossip; Contracts

The Page of Swords denotes useful information. Your hard work pays off in business and other work dealings. This is a time to be alert and observe carefully what others say. Be ready to take action as you see the right opportunity and consult others who can act as advocates on your behalf. This card often comes up to say that a contract will be coming your way—regarding property, careers, travel documents, and other agreements. This Page reminds you to rely on your intelligence.

What feelings does this card evoke in you?

_____

_____

_____

_____

Think about your current situation. Are you a curious person? What might you need to learn or ask for help on?

_____

_____

_____

_____

Focus and direction may not be your strong suit at the moment. New ideas, possibilities, dreams, and desires keep your head buzzing. You can try to harness that flow or follow it where it takes you. Write about those ideas here; don't limit yourself to proper sentences— just let it flow!

_____

_____

_____

Reversal: The reversed Page becomes manipulative and cunning. Be cautious about information you receive now, as it may not be reliable, and be discerning about what you hear about other people, as it may be unjust and even slanderous. Write about some gossip you've heard recently and whether you think it's true. Does it matter? Is it worth repeating? What do you think the gossiper's motive is?

_____

_____

_____

_____

Knight of Swords

CAUTION: ROCKY ROAD AHEAD

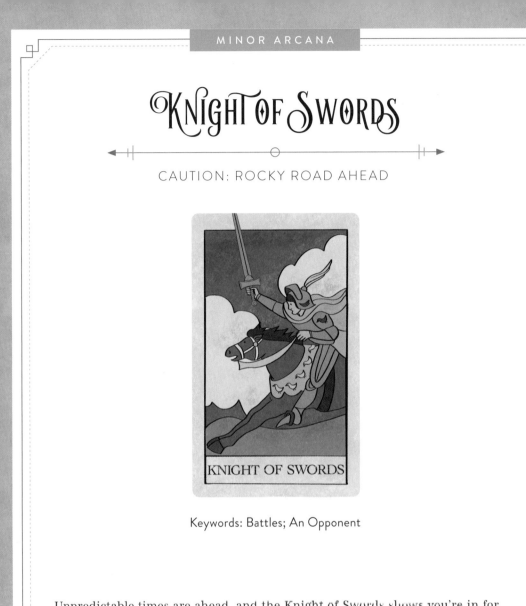

KNIGHT OF SWORDS

Keywords: Battles; An Opponent

Unpredictable times are ahead, and the Knight of Swords shows you're in for a drama of highs and lows. Sudden truths may come to light, or underlying conflicts may be exposed. The Knight often comes up to show disputes at work and tension within families and in romantic relationships. What counts now is how you recover. There is a way forward, but you may need to wait until the situation is calmer before you can make a move.

What feelings does this card evoke in you?

_____

_____

_____

_____

Has a truth or conflict been revealed to you recently? Though it may be sudden or difficult, write about what might be underlying the conflict and how you can move forward.

_____

_____

_____

_____

Confident in what you believe, you charge forward with conviction. Be certain about your course of action and look before you leap. Is that satisfaction from doing the right thing, or simply doing?

_____

_____

_____

Reversal: The reversed Knight means stressful situations are blown out of proportion as an individual thrives on drama but lacks the courage to take control. The card also advises that you may be let down by someone you thought was reliable and steadfast. Write about a "drama queen" in your life or someone who's let you down.

_____

_____

_____

_____

QUEEN OF SWORDS

LOOK AT THE BIG PICTURE

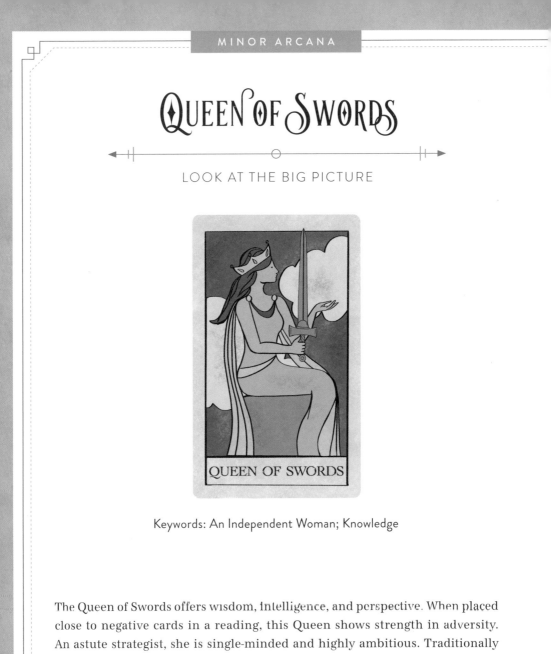

Keywords: An Independent Woman; Knowledge

The Queen of Swords offers wisdom, intelligence, and perspective. When placed close to negative cards in a reading, this Queen shows strength in adversity. An astute strategist, she is single-minded and highly ambitious. Traditionally this card is known as the widow but means in general a single woman or a woman who has to make her own way in the world. This card is a reminder to be determined and stand strong.

What feelings does this card evoke in you?

_____

_____

_____

_____

Think of a woman in your life who is strong and forthright, blunt but honest. How is she perceived by others, and are those positive perceptions or negative? Would those perceptions change if she were a man?

_____

_____

_____

Strength can be perceived as harshness, but it doesn't have to be. What you have gone through has given you wisdom, as well as independence, and a strong set of principles. Write about what you have learned.

_____

_____

_____

Reversal: The reversed Queen suggests excuses for bad behavior or a situation in which you are unjustly attacked. This individual can be an opponent or someone who has suddenly turned bitter and vengeful; she lacks awareness of just how unreasonable her demands have become. Write about a person like this (male or female) and the steps you can take to back away from them.

_____

_____

_____

_____

KING OF SWORDS

TAKE A TRIP TO YOUR MIND PALACE

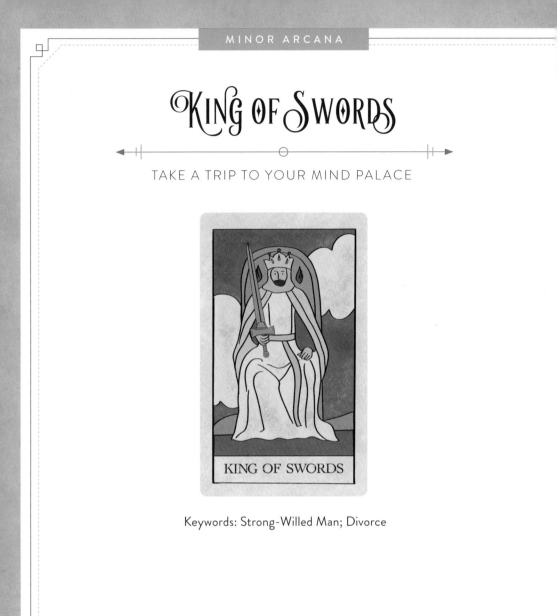

Keywords: Strong-Willed Man; Divorce

The King of Swords tells you to focus on the mind rather than the heart. It suggests intelligence, analysis, and authority, but also fairness and honesty. You may be going through an intensive time of work or study. In relationships and domestic affairs, it's time to take the initiative; a break-up might be on the horizon. Rely on logic to win.

What feelings does this card evoke in you?

_____

_____

_____

_____

Think of an emotionally charged situation you've been in. Were you (or the other person) able to remain rational, or did tempers flare?

_____

_____

_____

Being in charge can be as simple as just thinking it. Use that confidence to be decisive. Keep your standards high, and don't forget to show compassion. Write about a decision you need to make, writing out the pros and cons.

_____

_____

_____

Reversal: When reversed, the influence of the usually balanced King can be destructive. You may be put under unreasonable pressure to produce results. Unfortunately, there's no room for argument or personal interpretations, so you may feel oppressed. Thankfully, this is temporary. If you are dealing with someone who plays mind games and who will do almost anything to win, write about your feelings here.

_____

_____

_____

_____

ACE OF WANDS

GET READY FOR ADVENTURE!

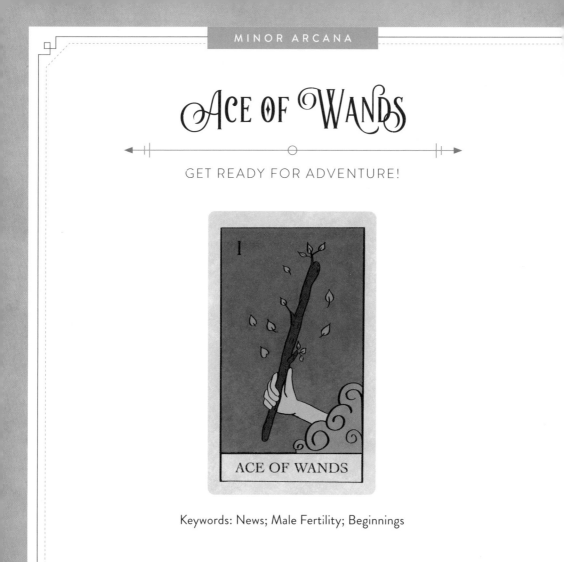

Keywords: News; Male Fertility; Beginnings

The Ace of Wands is auspicious for every aspect of your life. It predicts new beginnings, enterprise, and invention, and it often relates to work issues and projects. It's a happy card for creative work, too. With the Ace, you experience a flash of inspiration and know what to do next to give form to your concept. An additional meaning of the card is travel and adventure.

What feelings does this card evoke in you?

_____

_____

_____

_____

What excites you right now, whether it's a new project at work, a new relationship, or a trip in the planning?

_____

_____

_____

This is a good time to ponder the well of your inspiration. Do you have a deep and underlying passion? Now might be the time to follow it, as conditions may be well-suited for creation, invention, and even rebirth. Write about your passion and what you can do with it or about it—and what you might need to support those dreams.

_____

_____

_____

Reversal: The reversed Ace can show blocks to creative projects and delays to travel. It can reveal false starts; plans need a rethink. In work, a project may be abandoned or postponed due to poor management. In relationships, it might show a lack of commitment or time apart for a couple, usually due to work. Are you feeling blocked or delayed lately?

_____

_____

_____

_____

TWO OF WANDS

BOOK THAT TICKET

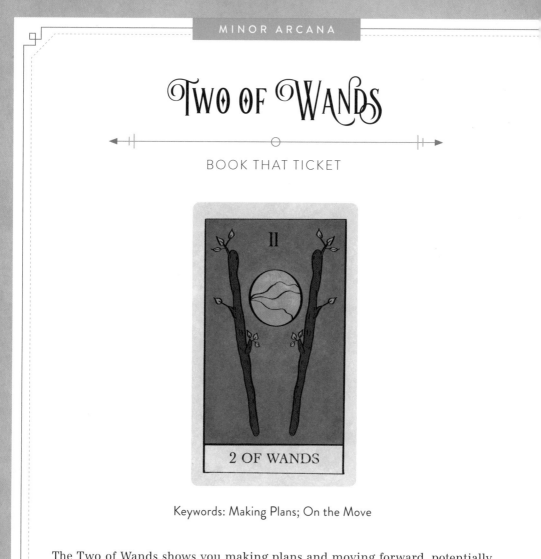

Keywords: Making Plans; On the Move

The Two of Wands shows you making plans and moving forward, potentially making travel arrangements. Great opportunities are on the way, allowing you to move up a level. In work, you are gaining influence and proving your worth; in return, you receive good support and advice. This Two can also show new creative partnerships and beginning a new enterprise. As there are two wands on the card, there are also two aspects to your situation. Consider what helps you on your path and any issues that hold you back. Make a plan that maximizes your strengths so your talent continues to shine.

What feelings does this card evoke in you?

_____

_____

_____

_____

Are you more of a planner or are you more spontaneous, and how has that worked out for you?

_____

_____

_____

_____

Everyone has goals. You have made some progress towards yours, but there is still some distance to go. Making plans for the next step of your journey can help. Write those plans here.

_____

_____

_____

Reversal: When the Two is reversed, your talent may be wasted because those who can help you progress are not listening. If this is the case, consider a change of scenery. The card can also show misplaced trust and an unreliable partner. Check if those close to you are pulling their weight—are you doing all the work?

_____

_____

_____

Three of Wands

LIVE YOUR BEST LIFE

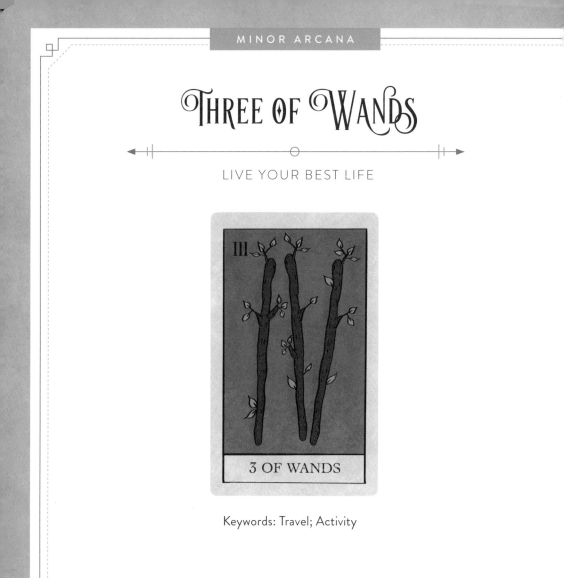

Keywords: Travel; Activity

The Three of Wands is a good-fortune card, predicting an intense period of activity. It reveals successful enterprise and seeing your projects and relationships thrive; it also indicates weddings, a new and important relationship, and an imminent trip. This is also a time for great communication and self-expression. This Three favors individuality and nonconformism. Pride yourself on your quirks and eccentricities, and let others see all you have to offer. Appreciate those around you; try to make time for friends who don't immediately fit into your future plans.

What feelings does this card evoke in you?

_____

_____

_____

It's a challenge to keep the balance between staying focused on the prize while remaining patient and calm. What kind of future investment are you currently waiting on, or what past investment are you enjoying the returns on now?

_____

_____

_____

You have been successful, but not everything has been taken care of, and there are still more challenges to come. Still, you are in a position of power and confidence, and you have good visibility for what is to come. What (or who) can help you achieve the kind of success that you have long dreamed of?

_____

_____

_____

Reversal: When reversed, the Three shows communication problems. Plans are delayed, and it may be difficult to make progress in your projects. You may find it hard to express yourself and understand what others are saying, making you feel needlessly isolated. Resist the frustration that this influence brings and go with a slower pace for a while. Overall, this is still a card of good fortune, even when reversed. You can still succeed. Write about some miscommunications your may be having.

_____

_____

_____

Four of Wands

SHARE YOUR LIGHT

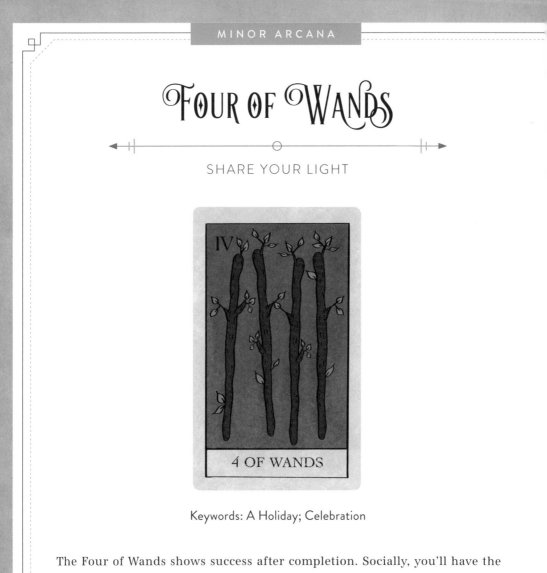

Keywords: A Holiday; Celebration

The Four of Wands shows success after completion. Socially, you'll have the opportunity to celebrate; you'll be brimming with confidence and vitality. Your talent is appreciated, and you're full of ideas and enthusiasm. You'll also establish yourself in your work and at home, completing a remodeling project or moving to a larger property. The vibe of this Four is putting down roots. Spiritually, it shows that you share your light with others. It often predicts that a new love interest will open their hearts and express affection. It's auspicious for creativity, and artistic projects flourish under this card's uplifting influence.

What feelings does this card evoke in you?

_____

_____

_____

_____

Is there an event you're involved in planning, even if it's just a small dinner party? Write down some ideas and organizational thoughts to get your ideas in motion.

_____

_____

_____

You have been on a journey and undergone significant change. Is it time for you to rest and recuperate? Find your place of refuge, whether with yourself or with beloved others. Consider what you've accomplished and write about that here.

_____

_____

_____

Reversal: The reversed Four retains its positive meaning, albeit with minor irritations. You don't get all the time you need to focus on doing what you love, and you may experience some disruption to plans. You might be feeling invisible and not heard. This unsettled phase will soon pass as the sunny aspect of the upright card prevails. Write about some delays or setbacks you've been experiencing.

_____

_____

_____

Five of Wands

HOLD YOUR POSITION

Keywords: Strong Opinions; Competition

The traditional meaning of the Five of Wands is competition, and the message is to hold your position rather than compromise. There will be fiery opinions and a lack of agreement, at least for now. Misunderstandings abound, particularly in work matters. Scheduling problems and delays to travel plans are an additional meaning. This Five often comes up to show being surrounded by people with strong opinions, particularly in families; in education, it predicts that you will need to compete hard, but you can succeed. On a lighter note, the card can also show competitions that are important to you.

What feelings does this card evoke in you?

_____

_____

_____

_____

How competitive are you, and is it a mental competitiveness that you keep to yourself, or do you go out there and make your voice or skills or opinions known?

_____

_____

_____

Be aware of the conflict and dissent in your life. These struggles can be highly disruptive but can also be a source of renewal. Looks for lessons in the strife. What can you learn?

_____

_____

_____

Reversal: The reversed Five shows deception and misinformation. You may be misled, so consider the source of messages before you make assumptions. In its most negative aspect, the card can show dishonesty. In general, the Five can show you feeling stressed and in a weak position; be selective about the people you choose to trust. Think about some of the messages you've recently received. Do you instantly believe them, even if they give you cause for doubt?

_____

_____

_____

_____

SIX OF WANDS

ENJOY YOUR SUCCESS

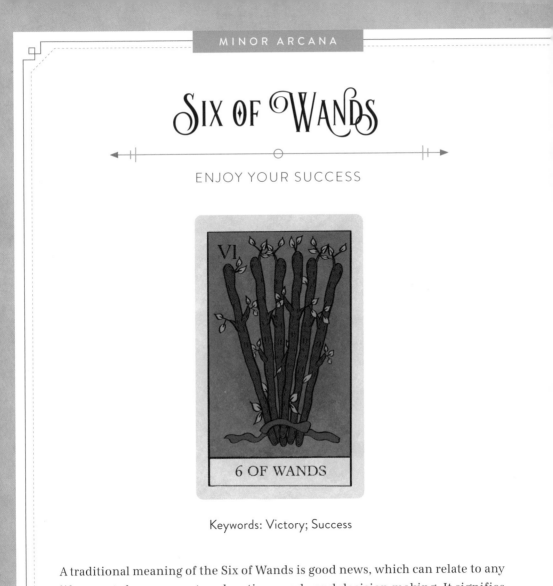

Keywords: Victory; Success

A traditional meaning of the Six of Wands is good news, which can relate to any life aspect—love, property, education, work, and decision-making. It signifies deserved success. The card often relates to work, career, and projects, and can show promotion and a new contract or bid; it can also reveal that a legal matter will go in your favor. Enjoy this happy time, regardless of how busy you are. In personal relationships, the card shows that feelings are declared—and will be well received. An additional meaning of this Six is celebrations, such as weddings and degree ceremonies.

What feelings does this card evoke in you?

_____

_____

_____

_____

How do you define success?

_____

_____

_____

_____

Things aren't perfect, but you've been able to marshal your skills and meet your goal. Take a moment to bask in your success. What did you do to accomplish your goal or surmount a difficulty?

_____

_____

_____

Reversal: With the reversed Six, the reward you've hoped for doesn't materialize when you need it to. But this is a card of delay rather than cancellation, so hold fast to your goals. Be patient. The card can also show you being let down by others, which dints your confidence, or pride, which can reveal an arrogant individual. Are you waiting for an overdue reward? Write about what you will do with it once it arrives.

_____

_____

_____

_____

Seven of Wands

FIGHT THE GOOD FIGHT

Keywords: Advocacy; Standing Strong

The Seven of Wands reveals obstacles in your path, but you will overcome them. It's particularly relevant to work and career matters and all negotiations. You'll need to stand tall and be clear on your position. This card often comes up to show you may be defending others, not just your own interests. In this sense, this Seven is the card of the advocate. Morality is important to you now, so you may become a group's spokesperson. In relationships, there are hurdles, and you may need to fight for love, provided you are sure your partner will return your loyalty.

What feelings does this card evoke in you?

_____

_____

_____

_____

What do you feel is worth standing up for, or what do you think you need to protect right now?

_____

_____

_____

_____

You've come a long way, and there's no possibility you'll turn back now. But are you feeling somewhat alone in your struggle, or are others working against you?

_____

_____

_____

_____

Reversal: When the Seven is reversed, you may doubt your purpose. You may struggle to be heard and have to overcome constant obstacles, and it's unclear the effort is worthwhile. The card can show anxiety, hesitation, and feeling overwhelmed. Focus on the areas where you can still make a difference, while accepting the things you cannot change; write about some of that here.

_____

_____

_____

_____

EIGHT OF WANDS

ENJOY THE EXCITEMENT

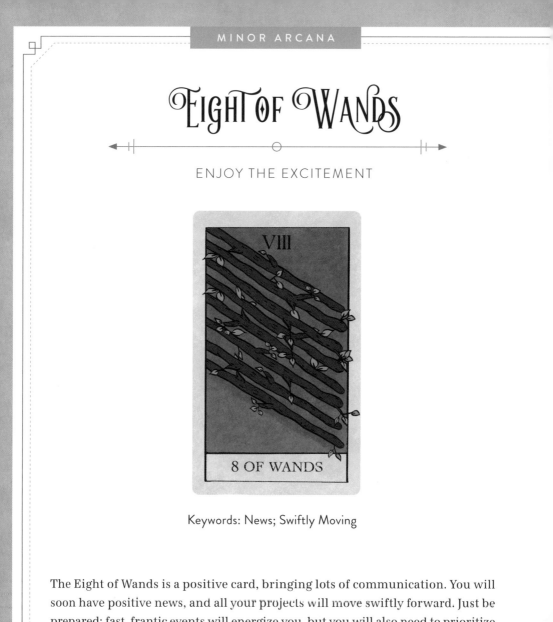

Keywords: News; Swiftly Moving

The Eight of Wands is a positive card, bringing lots of communication. You will soon have positive news, and all your projects will move swiftly forward. Just be prepared; fast, frantic events will energize you, but you will also need to prioritize any offers. Don't feel you have to say yes to everything. Choose wisely and enjoy this frenetic, exciting influence. In relationships, this Eight can bring great news about love, particularly if you've been separated from a partner or are waiting to hear from a potential partner; you may be traveling soon to see one another.

What feelings does this card evoke in you?

_____

_____

_____

_____

Think of someone you know who's constantly on the move. Does that lifestyle energize you or exhaust you? Why is that?

_____

_____

_____

Are you planning a trip? Either way, write down some thoughts about where you want to go, things you want to do and see, things you'd like to eat, souvenirs you'd like to buy.

_____

_____

_____

_____

Reversal: The reversed Eight means delay. You may have lots of pending work to finish, but for now, you'll need to be patient. It's also important to be discreet about any grievances you have. In relationships, you may be finding it hard to communicate. If you have hopes for a new love, you may be feeling disappointed by the person's lack of contact. An additional meaning is jealousy. Clear the air here by writing about grievances, jealous feelings, or disappointments.

_____

_____

_____

NINE OF WANDS

YOU CAN DO IT!

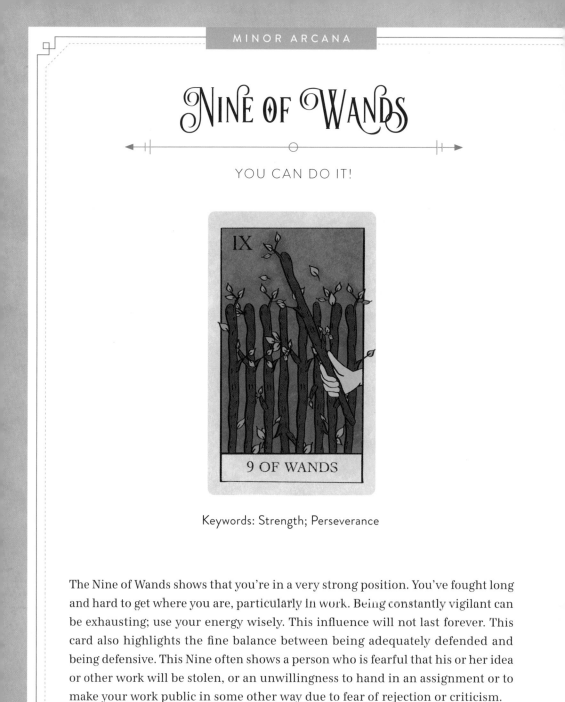

Keywords: Strength; Perseverance

The Nine of Wands shows that you're in a very strong position. You've fought long and hard to get where you are, particularly in work. Being constantly vigilant can be exhausting; use your energy wisely. This influence will not last forever. This card also highlights the fine balance between being adequately defended and being defensive. This Nine often shows a person who is fearful that his or her idea or other work will be stolen, or an unwillingness to hand in an assignment or to make your work public in some other way due to fear of rejection or criticism.

What feelings does this card evoke in you?

_____

_____

_____

Think of a goal you reached and the kind of adversity you had to overcome. Was it worth it? Would you do it again?

_____

_____

_____

It sometimes seems like if it isn't one thing it's another. You might feel as though your work never ends or that others are arrayed against you, but at the end of it all, you have what it takes to succeed. What are some of your current difficulties, and how can you overcome them?

_____

_____

_____

Reversal: With the reversed Nine, you endure strong opposition, which seems unfair. This situation is demotivating, so you become fixed on getting through tasks without enjoying your work. Equally, you could be the one who is obstinate and inflexible in your attitude. The card can also show issues with boundaries. Someone may be invading your territory—or you are veering into uncomfortable territory for them. Write about what this might mean to you.

_____

_____

_____

_____

TEN OF WANDS

JUST SAY NO

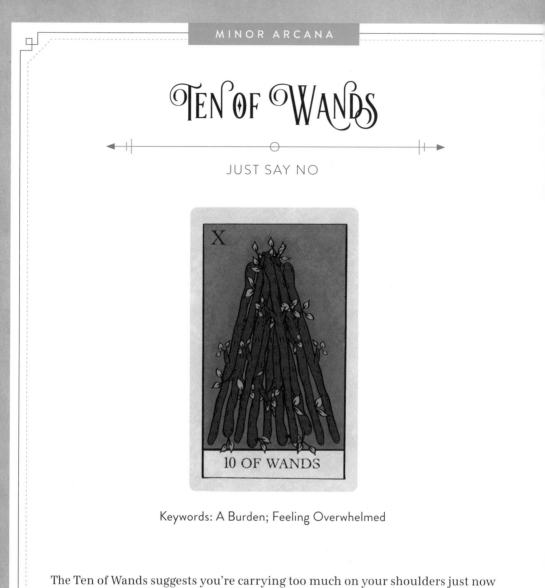

Keywords: A Burden; Feeling Overwhelmed

The Ten of Wands suggests you're carrying too much on your shoulders just now or that you may be carrying issues from the past. You may have become so used to being overloaded that you've lost sight of the reason you're doing the work. Consider saying no to future requests and decide which projects or jobs you can stop or hand over to someone else. There's a real need here for delegation and support from others. Burdens need to be shared. On a positive note, this Ten reveals that you can be successful with careful management of time and resources.

What feelings does this card evoke in you?

_____

_____

_____

_____

How do you feel about asking for help? How about delegating?

_____

_____

_____

_____

You might have been taking on too much. Is there something weighing on you? A responsibility that feels more like a burden?

_____

_____

_____

_____

Reversal: When the Ten is reversed, some burdens may be more perceived than real, which may be a sign of ongoing stress. Lighten up a little and take some of the pressure off yourself. You may also be caught in an exhausting grind between work and domestic commitments because you're trying to keep everyone happy. Make time for yourself. Obstinacy is one of the card's meanings, so ask yourself: have you have created too much self-pressure?

_____

_____

_____

_____

PAGE OF WANDS

USE THAT YOUTHFUL ENERGY

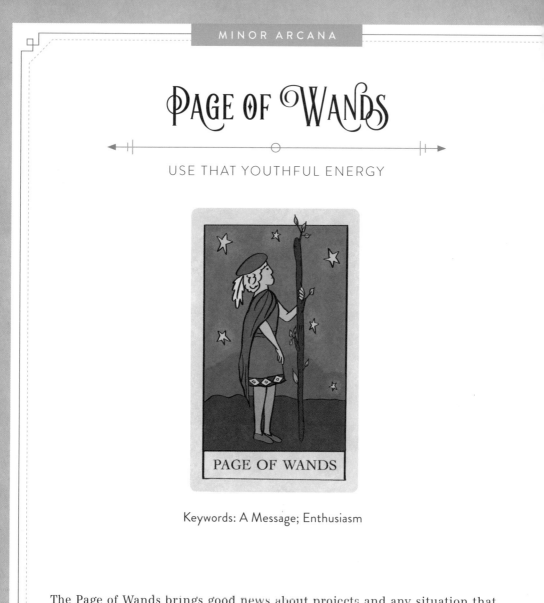

PAGE OF WANDS

Keywords: A Message; Enthusiasm

The Page of Wands brings good news about projects and any situation that requires negotiation. The atmosphere overall is one of trust, and you can rely upon information you receive. This Page can bring a creative enterprise or job offer—and, while the status of the job may not be as high as you might expect, the overall package may appeal. Check the details and practicalities before you agree to anything.

What feelings does this card evoke in you?

_____

_____

_____

Think of someone who always seems to be enthusiastic or motivated about things. How might you cultivate this same energy in your own life?

_____

_____

_____

Be open to that which is new and exciting. Recall the thrill (and the tension and uncertainty) that courses through you when you are about to set off on an adventure and write about something exciting that's on your horizon.

_____

_____

_____

Reversal: The reversed Page brings delays. Emails and other messages go astray, and communication gets complicated. The card can also show stubbornness and an inability to listen to others' opinions. This Page is fickle and doesn't follow through with what they start. An additional meaning is a child or young person struggling with written communication or speech. Do you know someone who just can't let a subject drop, who can't appreciate others' views, or who generally has trouble communicating?

_____

_____

_____

KNIGHT OF WANDS

PUT THE PEDAL TO THE METAL

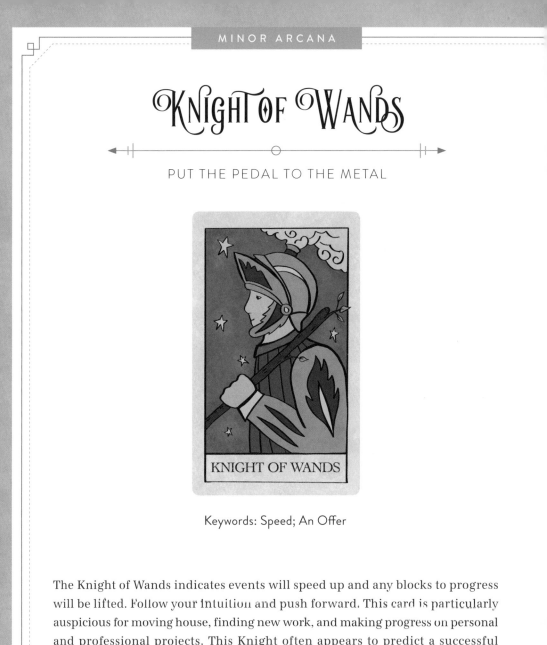

Keywords: Speed; An Offer

The Knight of Wands indicates events will speed up and any blocks to progress will be lifted. Follow your intuition and push forward. This card is particularly auspicious for moving house, finding new work, and making progress on personal and professional projects. This Knight often appears to predict a successful writing project. In other creative pursuits, you attract acknowledgment and support, both emotionally and financially. An additional meaning of the card is travel and emigration.

What feelings does this card evoke in you?

_____

_____

_____

_____

Are you experiencing a bit of wanderlust just now, or an urge to move to a new place?

_____

_____

_____

_____

You have what it takes to get things done. Let your enthusiasm and passion not only guide you but help you conquer your fears. But don't be careless! Make sure your energy takes you in the right direction. What are some things you'd like to accomplish?

_____

_____

_____

Reversal: The reversed Knight reveals a creative block or miscommunication—so emails go astray and other messages are not delivered. It also indicates delays and deferred decisions. This influence is temporary, but in the meantime, hold fast to your plans and your self-belief. As a person, this Knight is egotistical; they thrive on status but are generally unwilling to do any hard work to deserve it. What kind of delays are you experiencing?

_____

_____

_____

_____

QUEEN OF WANDS

STEP INTO YOUR POWER

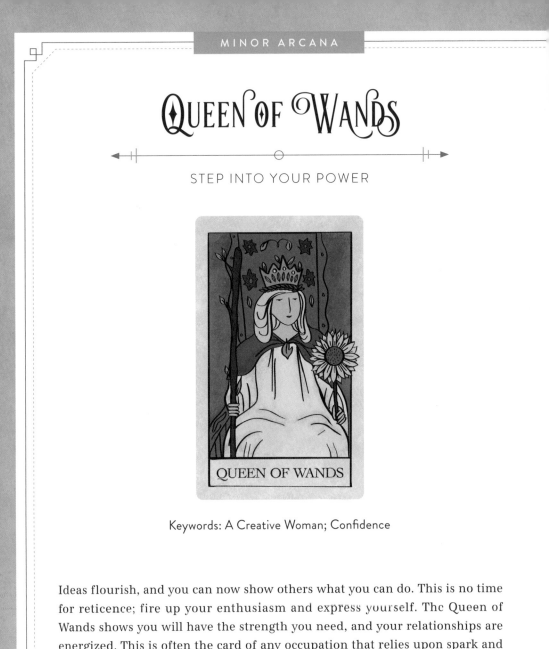

QUEEN OF WANDS

Keywords: A Creative Woman; Confidence

Ideas flourish, and you can now show others what you can do. This is no time for reticence; fire up your enthusiasm and express yourself. The Queen of Wands shows you will have the strength you need, and your relationships are energized. This is often the card of any occupation that relies upon spark and communication for success. Sociable and supportive, she is intensely loyal. This self-aware Queen is also in touch with her intuition, so she makes good choices in relationships. She often loves nature and animals, too.

What feelings does this card evoke in you?

_____

_____

_____

_____

What does loyalty mean to you?

_____

_____

_____

Your confidence is an asset, as is your luck. Charm, magnetism, and optimism bring others into your orbit. Listen to your nurturing side, but be careful not to give too much. How are you at balancing your needs with those of others?

_____

_____

_____

Reversal: When the Queen's reversed, you may feel controlled due to others' pointless interference. As a person, this Queen breaks promises. She can be envious and does not want anyone around her to shine more brightly. There is a great need for organization—but disorder rules. This may be because you, or someone close, has taken on too much and cannot admit it. Consider if this is a pattern—a way of avoiding being who you are, due to fear of rejection—and write about it here.

_____

_____

_____

_____

KING OF WANDS

BE A FREE SPIRIT

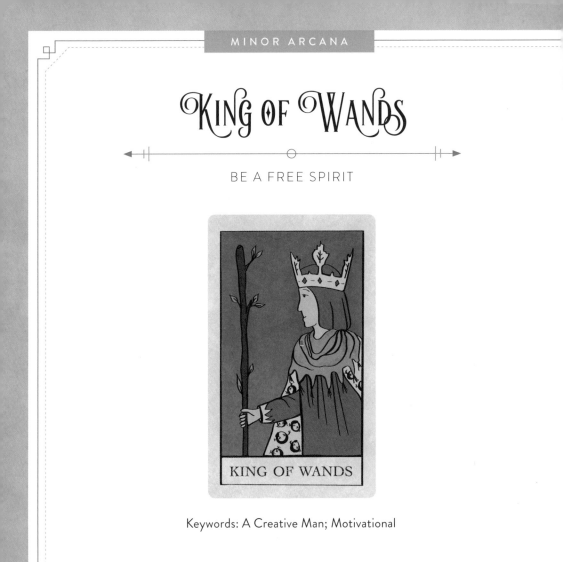

KING OF WANDS

Keywords: A Creative Man; Motivational

With the King of Wands, it is the right time to express your ideas and be who you are. Summon your entrepreneurial spirit and make a plan; what you propose will be well received and supported. Talkative and energetic, this King has wisdom, integrity, and high standards (for himself and others). Courteous and considerate, he stays true to his values and acts according to his moral code. He is self-aware and doesn't judge others; he often learns by listening to them. As a free spirit, he respects others who don't conform. As a potential partner, he is passionate and communicative.

What feelings does this card evoke in you?

_____

_____

_____

_____

 Has someone inspired you by sharing their experiences? Conversely, is there someone whom you've inspired?

_____

_____

_____

_____

There is a leader within you. When you point the way, others trust and follow. But what is your vision? Where are you taking them, or yourself? Write your plan here.

_____

_____

_____

Reversal: The reversed King indicates a time of restriction when you can't get others to see your point of view. Check that you're not going against your intuition and be open to alternative routes. Bullying, selfish, and opinionated, the reversed King as a person does not want to listen to anyone who doesn't agree with him; he is determined to get his own way. Does this describe someone you know (is it you?)?

_____

_____

_____

_____

The Spreads

The best way to get started is to just practice with your tarot cards. Spend a week or two shuffling your deck and going through the cards at random. Don't feel any need to think about what the designs mean. Clear your head and let your thoughts run free. Think in general terms about what you would like to talk to the cards about. Once you feel comfortable with your cards, you can have a better chance of hearing what they say to you. Some people like to write down impressions of the cards that they can refer to later, which you can do in this book.

After you have had your cards for at least a week or two and are feeling attuned to them, then you are ready to have your first reading. Prepare a good clean spot for conducting your readings. Your environment should reflect you. You can play music, but you should avoid clutter and distractions. The most important thing is that you are relaxed in the space and have enough room to lay out your cards. Where possible, try to use the same setting each time.

Tarot spreads are a designated pattern of cards in which each card position has a specific, predetermined meaning. There are almost infinite versions of tarot readings and spreads. Once a tarot spread is designed or selected, you can then shuffle your deck and begin pulling your cards for your reading. You can find tarot spreads in many books, on the internet, or through apps, and you can also design your own with a specific intention in mind. But you will find, over time, that you use two or three spreads regularly. Readers often learn the one-card daily reading (page 168); the three-card Past, Present, Future (page 174); the Celtic Cross (page 178); and the Week Ahead (page 184) as their foundation. Try them all and see which you prefer.

How to Read the Cards

First, shuffle the deck thoroughly. You can do this a few different ways:

1. Cut the deck by separating the cards into different stacks and then put those piles back together in a different order. (You may even feel the urge to do this a second time.)

2. Riffle the cards. This is what they call it when you split the deck in half, hold each half in a hand with your thumb on the bottom card and slowly release each side so they interleave; then with your thumbs on top, the cards fall back into place. This looks and sounds the coolest, but some people avoid it because it seems disrespectful to the cards.

3. Spread the cards out face-down on your cloth or any clean surface. Mix them all up with both hands. Bring them back together and stack them into a deck.

Repeat all or any of these as often as you like until the cards feel ready. The method doesn't really matter. The important thing is to not do it absent-mindedly but to be fully in the moment and attentive to the cards fluttering through your hands.

Cut the deck into smaller, even piles. Stack them back together. Identify a spread or intentional layout for the cards and what each position will indicate. When you feel the deck is ready, start selecting your card(s). Give yourself time to reflect on the questions you want to ask and allow the right cards for your reading to rise to the surface of the deck when it's time to pull them. When you're ready, pull the number and arrangement of cards that your spread calls for; they can either be pulled at random from the deck, off the top or bottom, or out of a jumble. Once you have your cards spread, turn them over horizontally, going left to right.

Now it's time to interpret and reflect! Humans are primed to recognize patterns and tell stories about themselves and others. Tarot draws on this innate ability to make connections, recognize ourselves in the stories around us, and reinterpret signs with meaning.

The One-Card Reading

Shuffle the deck, cut it or fan out the cards, and choose one card with your left hand. Think about a question you would like guidance on such as "What do I need to know today?" or "What am I not paying attention to?" or "What should I be focusing on?"

Date: _____

Question asked: _____

_____

Card drawn (note if upright ⬆ or reversed ⬇): _____

Keywords, themes, or symbols that come to mind: _____

_____

_____

_____

Interpretation and reflection: _____

_____

_____

_____

_____

_____

_____

_____

THE ONE-CARD READING

Shuffle the deck, cut it or fan out the cards, and choose one card with your left hand. Think about a question you would like guidance on such as "What do I need to know today?" or "What am I not paying attention to?" or "What should I be focusing on?"

Date: _____

Question asked: _____
_____

Card drawn (note if upright ↑ or reversed ↓): _____

Keywords, themes, or symbols that come to mind: _____
_____
_____
_____

Interpretation and reflection: _____
_____
_____
_____
_____
_____
_____
_____

THE ONE-CARD READING

Shuffle the deck, cut it or fan out the cards, and choose one card with your left hand. Think about a question you would like guidance on such as "What do I need to know today?" or "What am I not paying attention to?" or "What should I be focusing on?"

Date: _____

Question asked: _____
_____

Card drawn (note if upright ⬆ or reversed ⬇): _____

Keywords, themes, or symbols that come to mind: _____
_____
_____
_____

Interpretation and reflection: _____
_____
_____
_____
_____
_____
_____
_____

The One-Card Reading

Shuffle the deck, cut it or fan out the cards, and choose one card with your left hand. Think about a question you would like guidance on such as "What do I need to know today?" or "What am I not paying attention to?" or "What should I be focusing on?"

Date: _____

Question asked: _____
_____

Card drawn (note if upright ⬆ or reversed ⬇): _____

Keywords, themes, or symbols that come to mind: _____
_____
_____
_____

Interpretation and reflection: _____
_____
_____
_____
_____
_____
_____
_____
_____

THE ONE-CARD READING

Shuffle the deck, cut it or fan out the cards, and choose one card with your left hand. Think about a question you would like guidance on such as "What do I need to know today?" or "What am I not paying attention to?" or "What should I be focusing on?"

Date: _____

Question asked: _____

_____

Card drawn (note if upright ↑ or reversed ↓): _____

Keywords, themes, or symbols that come to mind: _____

_____

_____

_____

Interpretation and reflection: _____

_____

_____

_____

_____

_____

_____

_____

_____

The One-Card Reading

Shuffle the deck, cut it or fan out the cards, and choose one card with your left hand. Think about a question you would like guidance on such as "What do I need to know today?" or "What am I not paying attention to?" or "What should I be focusing on?"

Date: _____

Question asked: _____
_____

Card drawn (note if upright ↑ or reversed ↓): _____

Keywords, themes, or symbols that come to mind: _____
_____
_____
_____

Interpretation and reflection: _____
_____
_____
_____
_____
_____
_____
_____
_____
_____

Past, Present, Future Card Reading

This easy spread is perfect for mini-readings. Shuffle the cards and cut the deck, then draw the top card and place it in slot one, the next card in slot two, and the last in slot three. Or fan the cards and choose three that speak to you, then lay them as shown. Each card represents the designated time (past, present, future). Reflect on the cards, their relationship to one another, and your interpretation.

Date: _____

Question asked: _____

_____

_____

_____

_____

_____

❶	❷	❸
PAST	PRESENT	FUTURE
□↑ □↓	□↑ □↓	□↑ □↓

Card drawn (note if upright ↑ or reversed ↓):

1. Past: _____

2. Present: _____

3. Future: _____

Keywords, themes, or symbols that come to mind: _____

_____

_____

_____

Interpretation and reflection: _____

_____

_____

_____

_____

Past, Present, Future Card Reading

This easy spread is perfect for mini-readings. Shuffle the cards and cut the deck, then draw the top card and place it in slot one, the next card in slot two, and the last in slot three. Or fan the cards and choose three that speak to you, then lay them as shown. Each card represents the designated time (past, present, future). Reflect on the cards, their relationship to one another, and your interpretation.

Date: _____

Question asked: _____

_____

_____

_____

_____

1	**2**	**3**
PAST	PRESENT	FUTURE
□↑ □↓	□↑ □↓	□↑ □↓

Card drawn (note if upright ↑ or reversed ↓):

1. Past: _____

2. Present: _____

3. Future: _____

Keywords, themes, or symbols that come to mind: _____

_____

_____

_____

Interpretation and reflection: _____

_____

_____

_____

_____

Past, Present, Future Card Reading

This easy spread is perfect for mini-readings. Shuffle the cards and cut the deck, then draw the top card and place it in slot one, the next card in slot two, and the last in slot three. Or fan the cards and choose three that speak to you, then lay them as shown. Each card represents the designated time (past, present, future). Reflect on the cards, their relationship to one another, and your interpretation.

Date: _____

Question asked: _____

_____

_____

_____

_____

_____

❶ PAST □↑ □↓
❷ PRESENT □↑ □↓
❸ FUTURE □↑ □↓

Card drawn (note if upright ↑ or reversed ↓):

1. Past: _____

2. Present: _____

3. Future: _____

Keywords, themes, or symbols that come to mind: _____

_____

_____

_____

Interpretation and reflection: _____

_____

_____

_____

_____

Past, Present, Future Card Reading

This easy spread is perfect for mini-readings. Shuffle the cards and cut the deck, then draw the top card and place it in slot one, the next card in slot two, and the last in slot three. Or fan the cards and choose three that speak to you, then lay them as shown. Each card represents the designated time (past, present, future). Reflect on the cards, their relationship to one another, and your interpretation.

Date: _____

Question asked: _____

_____

_____

_____

_____

_____

❶	❷	❸
PAST	PRESENT	FUTURE
☐↑ ☐↓	☐↑ ☐↓	☐↑ ☐↓

Card drawn (note if upright ↑ or reversed ↓):

1. Past: _____

2. Present: _____

3. Future: _____

Keywords, themes, or symbols that come to mind: _____

_____

_____

_____

Interpretation and reflection: _____

_____

_____

_____

_____

THE CELTIC-CROSS

The Celtic Cross is one of most popular tarot spreads because it answers a question or, if you don't have an immediate question, gives an overview of your life just now. Set your intention before you begin, asking your question as your shuffle. Shuffle and choose the cards and then lay them out as shown. If the tenth card is a court card—a Page, Knight, Queen, or King—then the outcome of the question is up to you.

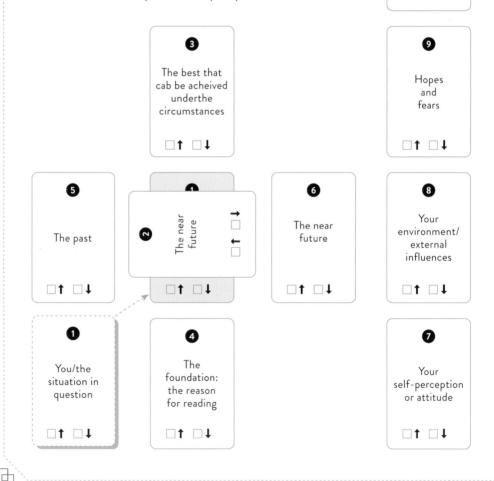

10 The outcome

3 The best that cab be acheived underthe circumstances □↑ □↓

9 Hopes and fears □↑ □↓

5 The past □↑ □↓

1 The near future → □ ← □

2

6 The near future □↑ □↓

8 Your environment/ external influences □↑ □↓

1 You/the situation in question □↑ □↓

4 The foundation: the reason for reading □↑ □↓

7 Your self-perception or attitude □↑ □↓

Date: _____

Question asked: _____

_____

Card drawn (note if upright ↑ or reversed ↓):

1. You/the situation in question: _____

2. What crosses or complements you: _____

3. The best that can be achieved in the circumstances: _____

4. The reason for the reading: _____

5. The past: _____

6. The near future: _____

7. Your self-perception or attitude: _____

8. Your environment/external influences: _____

9. Hopes or fears: _____

10. The outcome: _____

Keywords, themes, or symbols that come to mind: _____

_____

_____

_____

Interpretation and reflection: _____

_____

_____

_____

_____

_____

_____

_____

THE CELTIC-CROSS

The Celtic Cross is one of most popular tarot spreads because it answers a question or, if you don't have an immediate question, gives an overview of your life just now. Set your intention before you begin, asking your question as your shuffle. Shuffle and choose the cards and then lay them out as shown. If the tenth card is a court card—a Page, Knight, Queen, or King—then the outcome of the question is up to you.

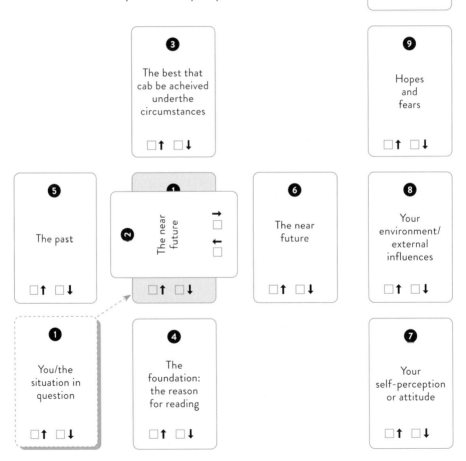

10 The outcome

3 The best that cab be acheived underthe circumstances □↑ □↓

9 Hopes and fears □↑ □↓

5 The past □↑ □↓

1 The near future → □ ← □

2

6 The near future □↑ □↓

8 Your environment/ external influences □↑ □↓

1 You/the situation in question □↑ □↓

4 The foundation: the reason for reading □↑ □↓

7 Your self-perception or attitude □↑ □↓

Date: _____

Question asked: _____
_____

Card drawn (note if upright ↑ or reversed ↓):

1. You/the situation in question: _____

2. What crosses or complements you: _____

3. The best that can be achieved in the circumstances: _____

4. The reason for the reading: _____

5. The past: _____

6. The near future: _____

7. Your self-perception or attitude: _____

8. Your environment/external influences: _____

9. Hopes or fears: _____

10. The outcome: _____

Keywords, themes, or symbols that come to mind: _____
_____
_____
_____

Interpretation and reflection: _____
_____
_____
_____
_____
_____
_____
_____

The Celtic-Cross

The Celtic Cross is one of most popular tarot spreads because it answers a question or, if you don't have an immediate question, gives an overview of your life just now. Set your intention before you begin, asking your question as your shuffle. Shuffle and choose the cards and then lay them out as shown. If the tenth card is a court card—a Page, Knight, Queen, or King—then the outcome of the question is up to you.

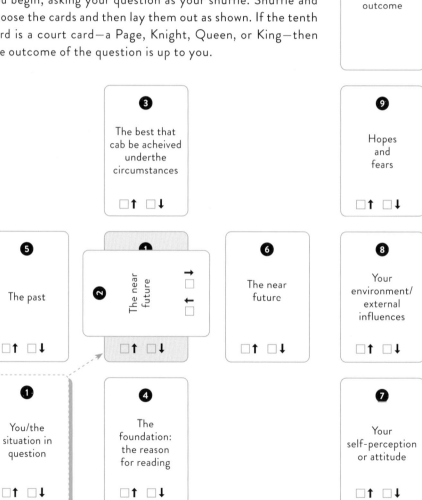

10 The outcome

3 The best that cab be acheived underthe circumstances

9 Hopes and fears

5 The past

1 The near future

2 The near future

6 The near future

8 Your environment/ external influences

1 You/the situation in question

4 The foundation: the reason for reading

7 Your self-perception or attitude

Date: _____

Question asked: _____
_____

Card drawn (note if upright ↑ or reversed ↓):

1. You/the situation in question: _____

2. What crosses or complements you: _____

3. The best that can be achieved in the circumstances: _____

4. The reason for the reading: _____

5. The past: _____

6. The near future: _____

7. Your self-perception or attitude: _____

8. Your environment/external influences: _____

9. Hopes or fears: _____

10. The outcome: _____

Keywords, themes, or symbols that come to mind: _____
_____
_____
_____

Interpretation and reflection: _____
_____
_____
_____
_____
_____
_____
_____

THE WEEK AHEAD

For a look at the week ahead, lay down one card for each day—though not in the regular, chronological sequence.

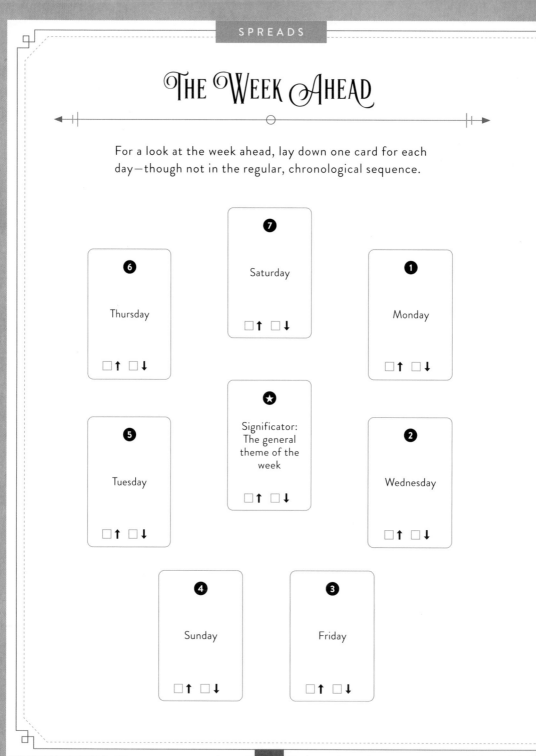

7 Saturday □↑ □↓

6 Thursday □↑ □↓

1 Monday □↑ □↓

★ Significator: The general theme of the week □↑ □↓

5 Tuesday □↑ □↓

2 Wednesday □↑ □↓

4 Sunday □↑ □↓

3 Friday □↑ □↓

Date: _____

Question asked: _____

_____

Card drawn (note if upright ⬆ or reversed ⬇):

1. Monday: _____

2. Wednesday: _____

3. Friday: _____

4. Sunday: _____

5. Tuesday: _____

6. Thursday: _____

7. Saturday: _____

★ Significator: The General Theme of the Week: _____

Keywords, themes, or symbols that come to mind: _____

_____

_____

_____

_____

_____

Interpretation and reflection: _____

_____

_____

_____

_____

_____

_____

THE WEEK AHEAD

For a look at the week ahead, lay down one card for each day—though not in the regular, chronological sequence.

7 Saturday □↑ □↓

6 Thursday □↑ □↓

1 Monday □↑ □↓

5 Tuesday □↑ □↓

★ Significator: The general theme of the week □↑ □↓

2 Wednesday □↑ □↓

4 Sunday □↑ □↓

3 Friday □↑ □↓

Date: _____

Question asked: _____
_____

Card drawn (note if upright ↑ or reversed ↓):

1. Monday: _____

2. Wednesday: _____

3. Friday: _____

4. Sunday: _____

5. Tuesday: _____

6. Thursday: _____

7. Saturday: _____

★ Significator: The General Theme of the Week: _____

Keywords, themes, or symbols that come to mind: _____
_____
_____
_____
_____

Interpretation and reflection: _____
_____
_____
_____
_____
_____
_____
_____

THE WEEK AHEAD

For a look at the week ahead, lay down one card for each day—though not in the regular, chronological sequence.

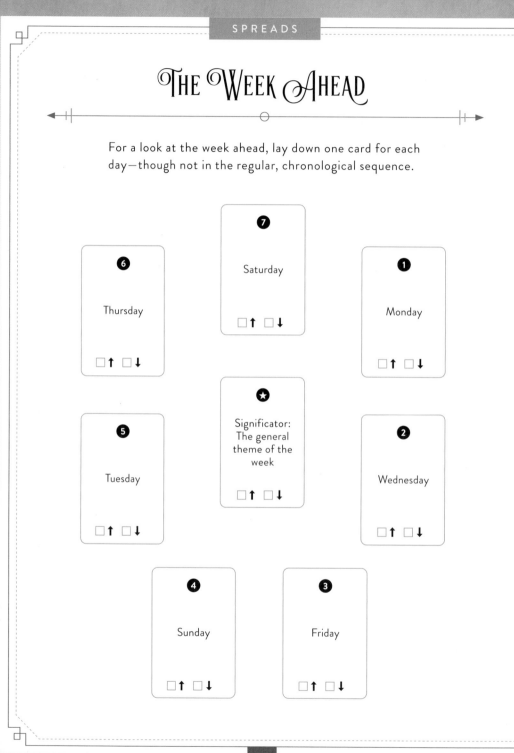

7 Saturday □↑ □↓

6 Thursday □↑ □↓

1 Monday □↑ □↓

5 Tuesday □↑ □↓

★ Significator: The general theme of the week □↑ □↓

2 Wednesday □↑ □↓

4 Sunday □↑ □↓

3 Friday □↑ □↓

Date: _____

Question asked: _____
_____

Card drawn (note if upright ↑ or reversed ↓):

1. Monday: _____

2. Wednesday: _____

3. Friday: _____

4. Sunday: _____

5. Tuesday: _____

6. Thursday: _____

7. Saturday: _____

★ Significator: The General Theme of the Week: _____

Keywords, themes, or symbols that come to mind: _____
_____
_____
_____
_____
_____

Interpretation and reflection: _____
_____
_____
_____
_____
_____
_____
_____

DIY SPREAD

To design a tarot spread of your own, you'll need to first select a topic or issue that you'd like to deal with. This can be a moon cycle, an image, or a series of questions you'd like to address. Draw out where you will lay the cards and label what the significance of each card's placement will be. You'll need to use this for reference and to hold yourself to the meaning of each card after you've shuffled and drawn your cards for the reading.

If you want to lay out a diamond-shape pattern and assign each card a different purpose every time, or put down a line of twelve cards corresponding to each month of the upcoming year, or jumble the whole deck together and read them randomly to accelerate the wisdom gained from accepting the seeming randomness of the universe (we call that one the Chaos Spread), go for it! What matters is that you focus on yourself, the card or cards in front of you, and let the truth flow through you. As long as you are being truthful about what you feel and telling that truth to yourself, then that is what matters. You can even shuffle and re-draw the cards if you do not get a feeling for the first one.

Be creative and experiment. Not all spreads you design will be useful, but with practice you will get a feel for what works for you. Dabble in as many spreads as you can from as many sources as possible and draw inspiration from your experimentation.

Sketch out your spread here